MERRY KNITMAS

– BY KNIT PICKS –

Copyright 2017 © Knit Picks

All rights reserved. This book or any portion thereof may not be reproduced or used in any manner whatsoever without the express written permission of the publisher except for the use of brief quotations in a book review.

Photography by Amy Cave

Printed in the United States of America

Second Printing, 2017

ISBN 978-1-62767-174-3

Versa Press, Inc
800-447-7829

www.versapress.com

CONTENTS

Introduction	4
Santa Pillow	6
Sweater & Stocking Ornaments	10
Snowdrift Blanket	18
Holiday Stockings	22
Nordic Star Pillow	26
Tiny Hearts	30
Snowflake Blanket	36
Townscape Pillow	40
Tannenbaum Tree Skirt	44
Festive Fair Isle Ornaments	48
Snow Star Pillow	52
Cable Sweater for Coffee Mug	56
Nordic Stocking	60
Snowflake Ornaments	66

INTRODUCTION

From wreaths and centerpieces, to cookies and pies, the holidays seem to bring out the maker in all of us. Far from the bright and busy days of summer, the blustery dark of winter inspires us to make our own warmth and light, cuddling together in our homes with cozy camaraderie.

Few can approach this time with the singular appreciation of a knitter. From that first hint of crisp autumn, we can hardly wait to pull out our cedar-packed sweaters and shawls, and limber up our fingers for the real knitting season. For we speak in fiber. Our affection and care is stitched in scarves and hats. Our joy and jubilation in stockings and blankets.

It seems a universal instinct to brighten and beautify your home for those long months, but there's a special kind of glow that comes from decking your halls with knits of your very own. From knitters to knitters, we offer these patterns to help you celebrate of this special time of year as only our fiber friends can. Make your own *Merry Knitmas*, stitch by stitch.

SANTA PILLOW
by Kathy Lewinski

FINISHED MEASUREMENTS
20" square

YARN
Knit Picks Wool of the Andes Worsted (100% Peruvian Highland Wool; 110 yards/50g): C1 Cranberry 23425, C2 White 24065; 4 balls each, C3 Oyster Heather 24649, C4 Coal 23420; 1 ball each

NEEDLES
US 6 (4mm) 32" circular needles, or size needed to obtain gauge

NOTIONS
Yarn Needle
Stitch Marker
20x20" Pillow Insert

GAUGE
22 sts and 26 rows = 4" in stranded St st in the round, blocked.

Santa Pillow

Notes:

A minimalist pattern of triangles and squares turns into rows of whimsical Santas, inspired by the Swedish Tomte.

This pillow is worked in the round with the same chart used for the front and back. The eyes may be knit while working the whole pattern, or duplicate stitched on afterwards.

The top of the pillow is finished in Kitchener stitch and the bottom is seamed together after a pillow inserted has been added.

This cover fits very snugly on a 20" pillow insert. Pillow inserts have a variety of densities; be sure to check your insert size compared to the finished project to make sure your stitches aren't stretched.

The chart is worked in the round, read each row from right to left as a RS row.

Jogless Color Work for Knitting in the Round

Working in the round creates a jump or jog in the color work pattern at the beginning of a round whenever the color is changed. This can be minimized by using the following technique.

Rnd 1 when starting new color on the first st: K normally.
Rnd 2: Before knitting the first st, bring the st from the rnd below up onto the left needle. Knit together with the first st of the rnd. Rep every time you change colors on the first st of a row.
For a video demonstration of how to work Kitchener st, see http://tutorials.knitpicks.com/wptutorials/kitchener-stitch

DIRECTIONS

CO 216 sts with C1, leaving a very long tail for seaming. Join together to knit in the rnd being careful not to twist sts. PM between the last and first st to mark beginning of rnd.
Rnds 1-52: K working Chart A eighteen times across each rnd.
Rnds 53-90: Rep rnds 15-52.
Rnds 91-129: K working Chart B eighteen times across each rnd.
Graft top closed, using Kitchener Stitch and C2.

Finishing

Duplicate Stitch eyes in C4 Coal yarn if not worked in while knitting.

Weave in ends and block.

Fill with pillow insert and seam the cast on edge together with C1.

Chart A

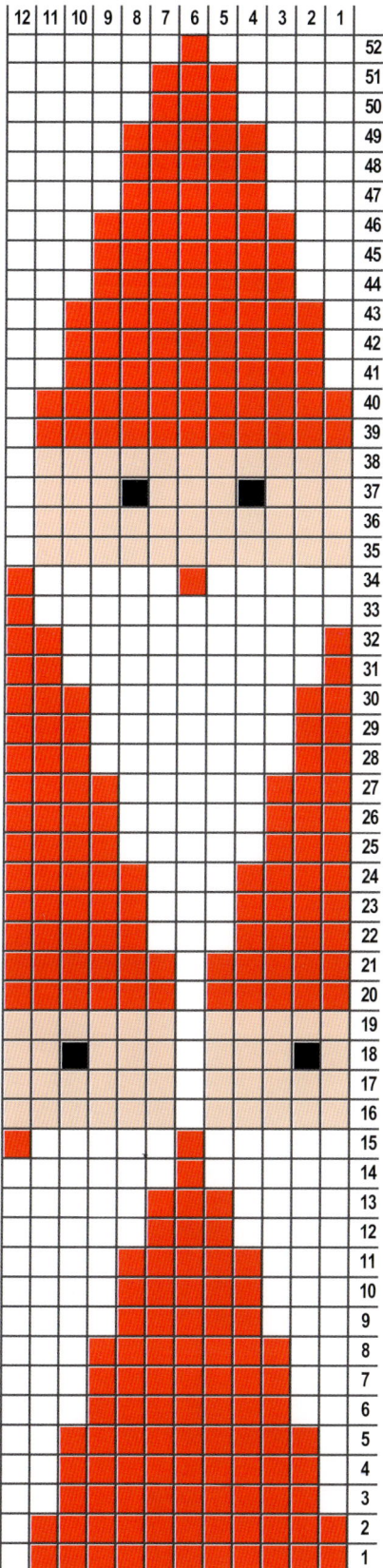

Legend:

☐ knit
knit stitch

■ C1

☐ C2

▨ C3

■ C4

Chart B

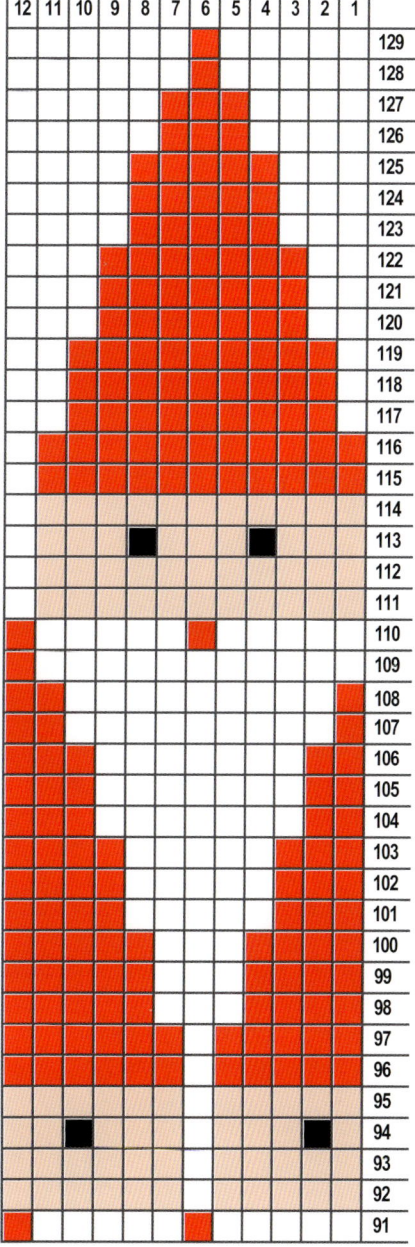

Santa Pillow 9

SWEATER & STOCKING ORNAMENTS

by Karen DiTommaso

FINISHED MEASUREMENTS

Sweater Ornaments: 3" high x 5" wide from sleeve to sleeve
Stocking Ornaments: 5.5" high from toe to top of hanger x 2.5" wide overall

YARN

Knit Picks Palette (100% Peruvian Highland Wool; 231 yards/50g): Cream 23730, Garnet Heather 24015, Forest Heather 24584, 1 skein each

NEEDLES

US 3 (3.25mm) DPNs or circular needles, or 1 size larger than size to obtain gauge

US 2 (2.75mm) DPNs or circular needles, or size to obtain gauge

NOTIONS

Crochet Hook US size D (3-3.25mm)
Yarn NeedleStitch Markers (3)
Bobbins for color work (optional)
Stitch Holders

GAUGE

26 sts and 36 rows = 4" in stranded St st on smaller needles, blocked. (Gauge for this project is approximate)

For pattern support, contact handmademaryellen@outlook.com

Sweater & Stocking Ornaments

Notes:

K1, P1 Rib (worked flat over multiples of 2 sts)
Row 1: *K1, P1; rep from * to end of row.
Rep Row 1 for pattern.

Stockinette Stitch (St st, worked flat)
Row 1 (RS): K.
Row 2 (WS): P.
Rep Rows 1-2 for pattern.

Garter Stitch
Row 1: Knit.
Rep Row 1 for pattern.

SWEATER ORNAMENTS

Notes: One Sweater Ornament pattern that can be knit with four different variations. Knit from the top down, using a fanciful yoke or an intarsia knitted design as you go. A little quick seaming and your sweater ornament is ready to decorate your tree or holiday gift.

Sweater Ornaments are knitted flat from the neck downwards. Charts are shown 'upside down' as you knit in that direction. RS chart rows are knitted and read from right to left. WS rows are purled and read from left to right. Refer to chosen chart to determine yarn color.

Ribbing
Using larger needles and Row 1 color of chosen chart, CO 32 sts using the Long Tail method.
Rows 1-2: Change to smaller needle, work in K1, P1, Rib.
Row 3 (WS): Working in K1, P1 Rib, PM after 11 sts, then 5 sts, then 11 sts, then work final 5 sts to end. 4 sections created.

Yoke
Begin chosen Sweater Chart on RS Row 4, following color changes as indicated.
The following instructions duplicate the charts, but do not include the color changes.
Row 4 (RS): *KFB, K to 1 st before M, KFB; SM, rep from * across. 8 sts inc, 2 sts per section.
Row 5 (WS): Purl.
Rows 6-11: Repeat Rows 4-5 three times. 64 sts.
Row 12: Rep Row 4. 72 sts. 21, 15, 21, 15 sts per section.

Body
Row 13 (WS): Removing stitch markers, P across 21 sts of first body section (back), place next 15 sts of sleeve section on stitch holder, P across 21 sts of second body section (front), place remaining 15 sts on stitch holder for second sleeve.
Rows 14-23: Work in St st.
Rows 24-26: Work in K1, P1 Rib.BO in K1, P1 Rib pattern.

Sleeves (make 2 the same)
The following instructions duplicate the Sleeve Length Detail chart. Place 15 held sts on smaller needles, ready to begin a WS row, continuing with same color.

Rows 1, 3 (WS): Purl.
Row 2 (RS): Knit.
Row 4: SSK, K across to last 2 sts, K2tog. 13 sts. Rows 5-9: Work in St st.
Rows 10-11: Work in K1, P1 Rib. *K1, P1* K1Row 12: BO in K1, P1 Rib pattern.

Finishing
Weave in loose ends in the design work on WS and trim, leaving CO and BO tails for seaming.

Give the sweater a steam by spraying both sides with spring or distilled water and press both sides with a hot iron. For best results, use a clean white dishcloth as a pressing cloth, ironing the WS first and making sure to uncurl the edges. This plumps up the sts and gives a nice smooth finish.

Sew seams for Sleeves, Back Yoke then Body Side, using tails from CO and BO.

Weave in remaining ends.

STOCKING ORNAMENTS

Notes: A fun to make Stocking Ornament pattern knit from the top down with a pine tree or reindeer intarsia design, knitted as you go. Once the knitting is done, a little simple overhand stitching sews up into the cutest little stocking for your tree, gift tags, or anywhere else that needs a little holiday festive touch.

Stocking Ornaments are knit flat from the cuff down to the toe. Charts are shown 'upside down' as you knit in that direction. RS chart rows are knit and read from right to left, WS rows are purled and read from left to right. Refer to chart Key to determine colors.

Both of the stocking ornaments are identical from the heel down to the toe (25 sts left on needle) with separate charts provided for each design.

Cuff
Using larger needles and color indicated on Row 1 of chosen chart, CO 33 sts using the Long Tail method. Leave a 24" tail for the crocheted hanger loop.
Rows 1-4: Work in Garter Stitch.
Cut yarn leaving a 6" tail to use when sewing up the finished stocking.

Leg
Begin chosen Stocking Chart on RS Row 5, following color changes as indicated.
The following instructions duplicate the charts, but do not include the color changes.

Row 5 (RS): Change to smaller needles and St st. With color indicated, K.

Pine Tree Stocking
Rows 6-27: Work Chart in St st. 25 sts.
Rows 21, 23, 25, 27 (decrease rows): K1, k2tog-tbl, K to last 3 sts, k2tog. 2 sts dec.

Reindeer Stocking

Rows 6-25: Work Chart in St st. 25 sts.

Rows 19, 21, 23, 25 (decrease rows): K1, k2tog-tbl, K to last 3 sts, k2tog. 2 sts dec.

Cut and tie off main color, leaving 12" tail to use for seaming.

Left Heel

With WS facing attach Cuff color, leaving a 6" tail for seaming.

Row 1 (WS): P7 and turn, leaving remaining sts on needle.

Row 2 (RS): Sl 1 st, K6.

Row 3-8: Rep Rows 1 - 2 three more times until 8 rows of heel have been worked.

Row 9: P3, P2tog, P1, turn leaving 1 remaining st of heel on needle.

Row 10: Sl 1, K4.

Row 11: P2, P2tog, turn leaving remaining 2 sts on needle. Row 12: Sl 1, K2.

Row 13: P2, P2tog, P1, turn.

Row 14: Sl 1, K3.

Cut yarn leaving an 8" tail that will be used when sewing up the heel of finished stocking.

Slide all the work along needle, turn with WS facing and resume working the Right Heel.

Right Heel

With RS facing, attach Cuff color.

Row 1 (RS): K7 and turn, leaving remaining sts on needle. Row 2 (WS): Sl 1, P6.

Row 3-8: Rep Rows 1 - 2 three more times until 8 rows of heel have been worked.

Row 9: K3, K2tog TBL, K1, turn leaving 1 remaining st of heel on needle.

Row 10: Sl 1, P4.

Row 11: K2, K2tog TBL, turn leaving remaining 2 sts on needle.

Row 12: Sl 1, P2.

Row 13: K2, K2tog TBL, K1, turn.

Row 14: Sl 1, P3, leaving these 4 sts on needle. 19 total sts.

Foot

With RS facing, rejoin MC.

Row 1 (RS): K across 4 sts of heel, PU 5 sts evenly from inside edge of heel. Continue with Row 1, K11 sts across main part of stocking, PU 5 sts from inside edge of 2nd heel half and K final 4 sts. 29 sts.

When picking up the 5 sts, PU 3 sts within the heel and then 1 st on each side of the MC.

Row 2 (WS): Purl.

Row 3: K8, K2tog, K9, K2tog TBL, K8. 27 sts. Row 4: P7, P2tog TBL, P9, P2tog, P7. 25 sts.

Row 5: K6, K2tog, K9, K2tog TBL, K6. 23 sts.

Rows 6-9: Work in St st.

Cut and tie off MC yarn, leaving 6" tail to use for seaming.

Toe Shaping

With RS facing, change to Cuff color for toe cap.

Row 1: Knit. Row 2: Purl.

Row 3: K2, K2tog TBL, K4, K2tog, K3, K2tog TBL, K4, K2tog, K2. 4 sts dec sts.

Rows 4-5: Rep Rows 2-3. 15 sts.

Row 6: Purl.

Cut and tie off yarn, leaving 7" tail.

Thread tail through the 15 sts using a yarn needle, pulling tight to evenly gather.

Finishing

Blocking

Weave in loose ends on WS and trim, leaving long tails as specified for seaming.

Give the stocking a steam by spraying both sides with spring or distilled water and press both sides with a hot iron. I use a clean white dishcloth as a pressing cloth, ironing the WS first and making sure to uncurl the edges. This plumps up the sts and gives a nice smooth finish.

Sewing Stocking

Fold the stocking WS out to sew the seam. Use a simple overhand st with the long tails, catching both loops of the edge sts, taking 1 st per row with the same color yarn used for each area and tie up the stitching yarn with a double knot at the end of each section with the 'other' tail of the same color.

Start at the top of the heel sewing up the leg, knotting the design yarn at the top.

Next, seam the cuff upwards tail from the end of Row 4, take a good secure stitch at the very top of the stocking and sew back downwards giving the seam a little extra stability to help it hang nicely. Finish the tail down the leg wrapping around the leg tails. Then, sew the heel and foot upwards.

For the toe, use the yarn that runs through the last row of sts, pulling it tight to gather.

Once completely sewn, trim the ends to tie up all ends securely and trim to about .75", there is no need to sew them in.

Turn RS out.

Hanging Loop

Using crochet hook and the long CO tail, chain stitch 16 sts and single crochet stitch to top of cuff just to the other side of the seam. Secure yarn to cuff and run a whip stitch about 2" down the back seam and trim.

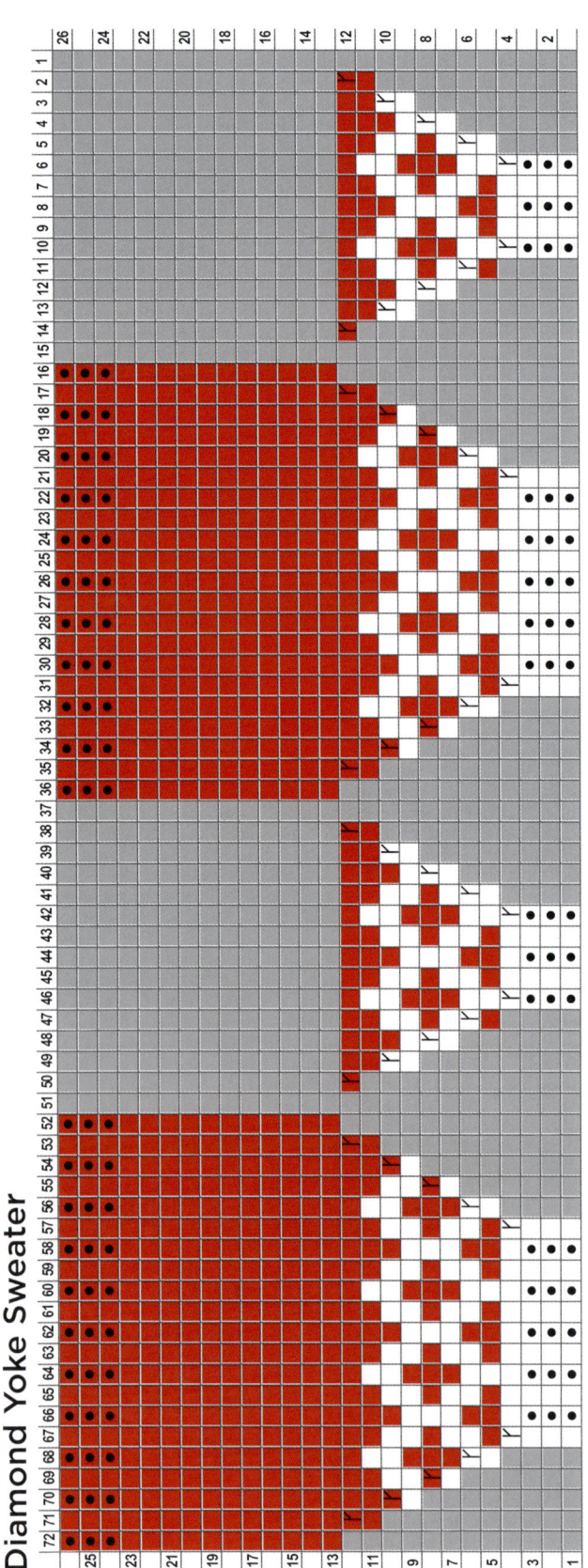

Diamond Yoke Sweater

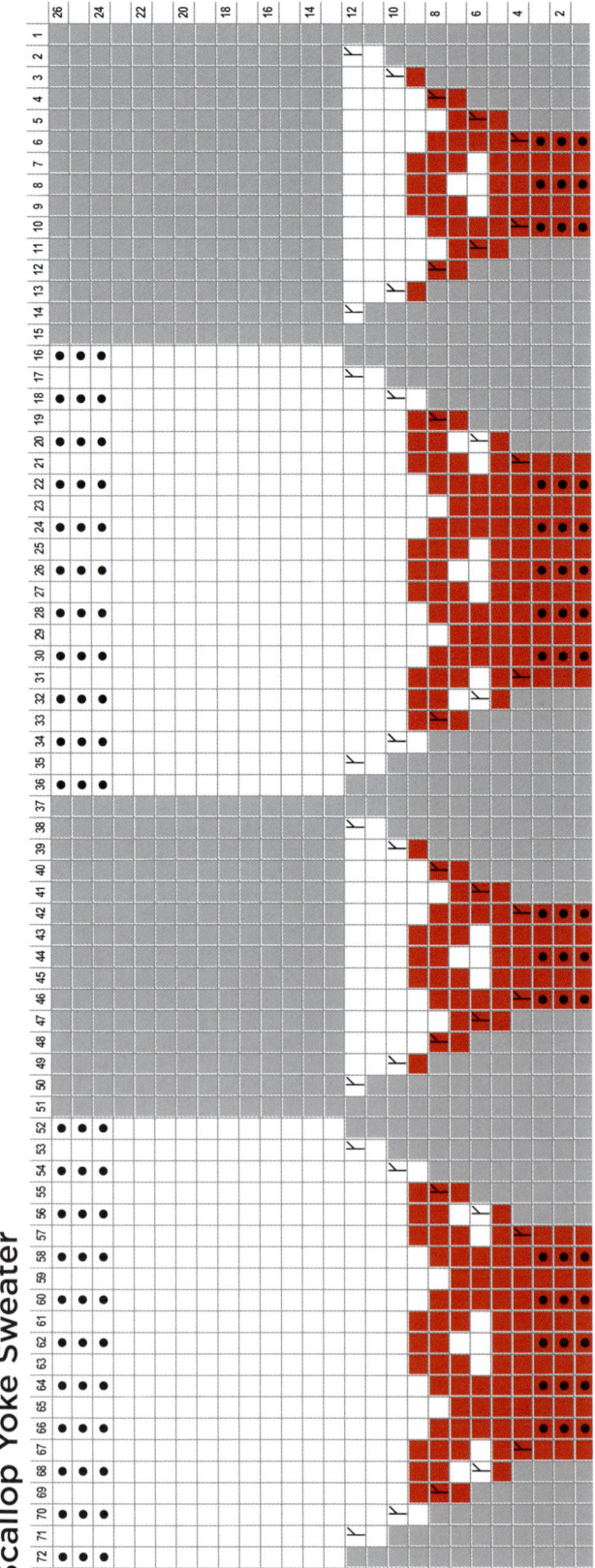

Scallop Yoke Sweater

14 Sweater & Stocking Ornaments

Sleeve Detail

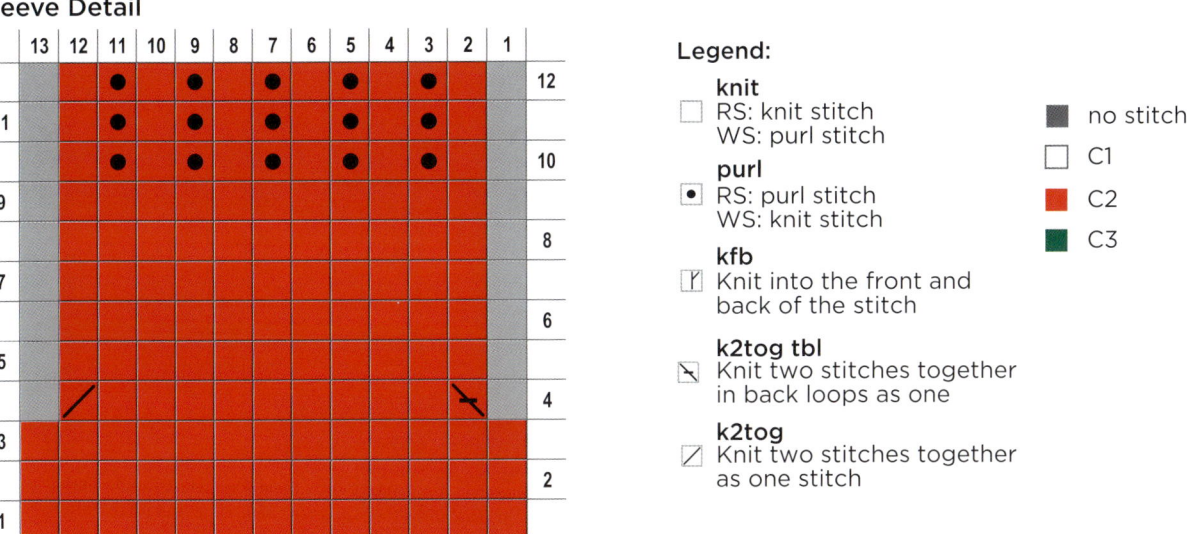

Legend:

knit
☐ RS: knit stitch
WS: purl stitch

purl
⦁ RS: purl stitch
WS: knit stitch

kfb
Knit into the front and back of the stitch

k2tog tbl
Knit two stitches together in back loops as one

k2tog
Knit two stitches together as one stitch

■ no stitch
☐ C1
■ C2
■ C3

Sweater & Stocking Ornaments 15

Reindeer Stocking

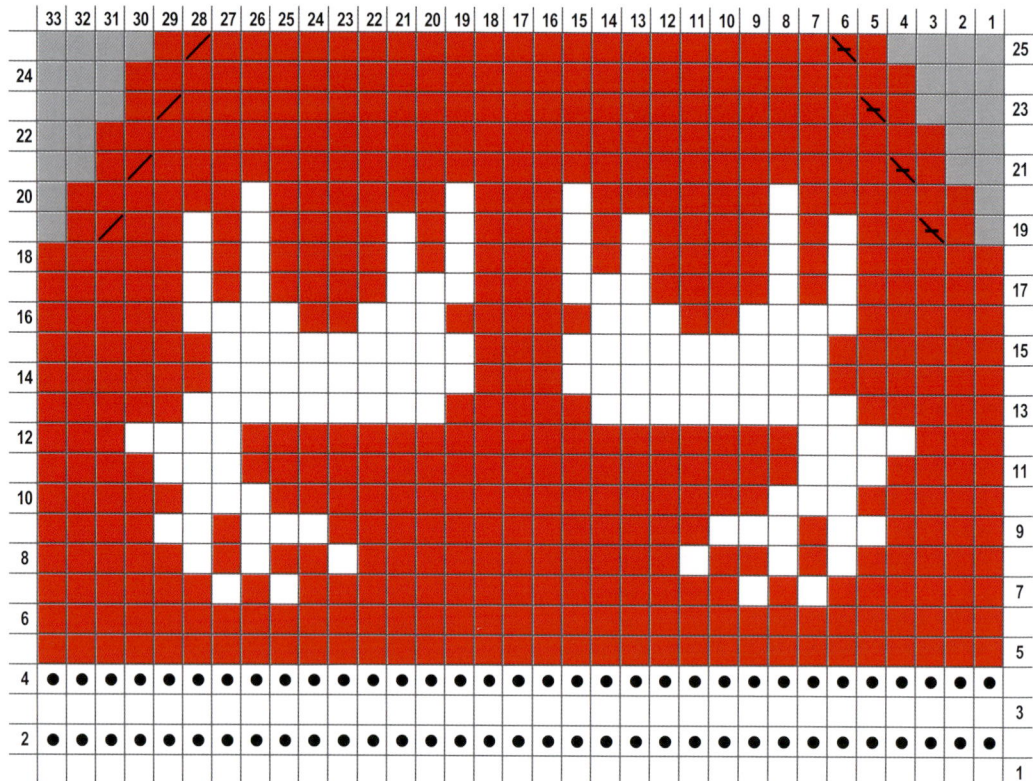

Pine Tree Stocking

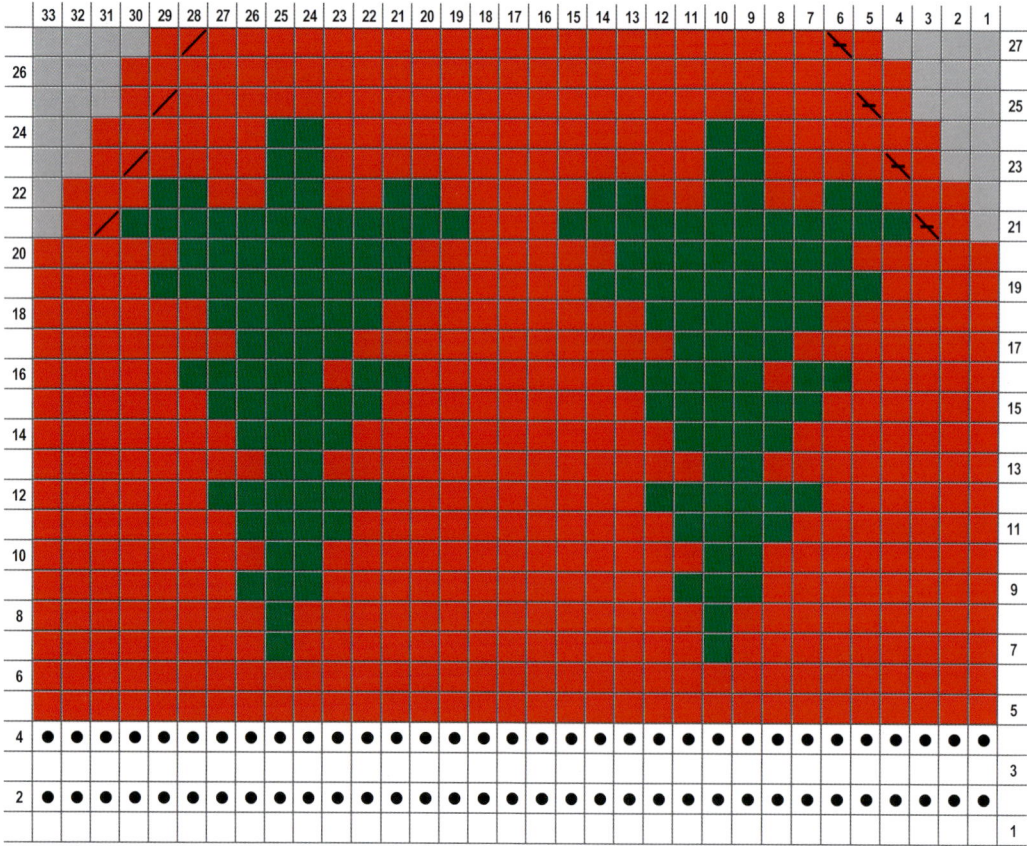

16 Sweater & Stocking Ornaments

Reindeer Sweater

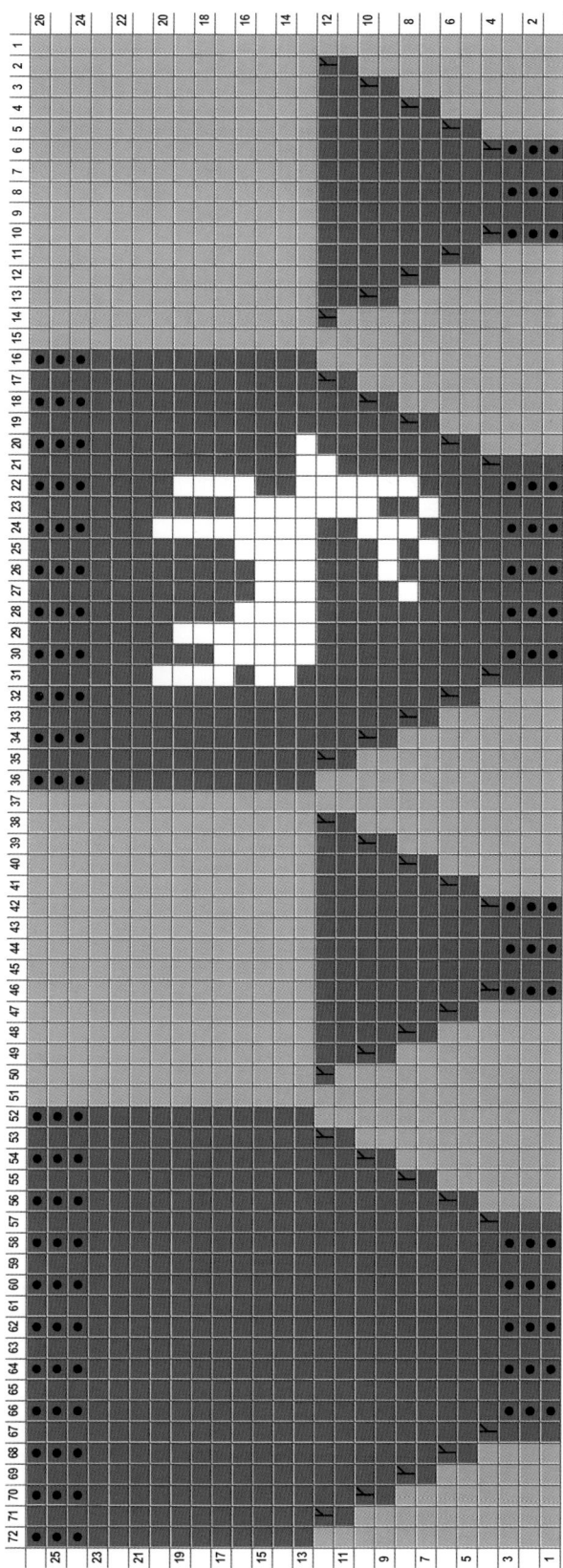

Snowflake Sweater

Sweater & Stocking Ornaments 17

SNOWDRIFT BLANKET

by Margaret Holzmann

FINISHED MEASUREMENTS
S (M, L, XL): 55 (65, 74, 84)" high x 41 (49, 56, 63)" wide

YARN
Knit Picks Mighty Stitch Worsted (80% Acrylic, 20% Superwash Wool; 208 yards/100g): MC Spruce 26826, 3 (5, 7, 8) balls; C1 Cream 26831, 2 (3, 4, 4) balls

NEEDLES
US 7 (4.5mm) 40" or longer circular needles, or size to obtain gauge

NOTIONS
Sewing Machine or H-8 (5mm) Crochet Hook
Sewing Pins
Yarn Needle
10 (12, 14, 16) Stitch Markers; half of one color or style and half of a different color or style
1.5, (3, 3.5, 4) yards of 45" wide cotton flannel, machine washed and dried
Polyester blend thread to match MC

GAUGE
19.5 sts and 20 rows = 4" in stranded St st in the rnd, blocked.

Snowdrift Blanket

Notes:
This blanket is worked in the round and uses a 'knitted steek,' which is a border of extra stitches which is reinforced after the blanket face is knitted, then cut and folded under, to be hidden behind the fabric backing. The knitted Seed stitch side borders are added via picked up sts after the steeks are cut.

The chart is worked in the round, read each row from right to left as a RS row. Change colors as indicated.

When a yarn must be carried more than four stitches at the back of the work, twist the MC and contrast yarns every fourth stitch. This practice maintains proper tension in the fabric. For long carries, alternate twist direction to keep the yarns from tangling.

DIRECTIONS

Body
Instructions for larger blanket sizes are in parentheses.

Bottom Border (worked flat)
CO 145 (174, 203, 232) sts.
Row 1 (WS): *K1, P1; rep from * across row.
Row 2 (RS): K the P sts, and P the K sts.
Rows 3-12: Rep Rows 1 - 2, five more times, for a total of 12 rows of Seed stitch.
Row 13 (inc row): P1 (1, 2, 2), *PFB P3; rep from * 36 (43, 50, 57) times, P0 (1, 1, 2). 181 (217, 253, 289) sts.

Blanket Face (worked in the rnd)
On the first row, PM on the 19th st then every 18th st thereafter across the row. Use one color to mark the center of each snowflake and another color or style to mark the midpoint between snowflakes.
Row 14 (RS): CO 11 sts at the beginning of the row onto the LH needle. P1, K9, P1 across these sts, then PM on the needle. These are the 'steek' sts and are not shown on the chart. Begin Row 14 of the Snowdrift Blanket chart, making 5 (6, 7, 8) reps of columns 1-36 of the chart across the rnd, and ending with column 37 of the chart. Do not turn.
Rnd 15: Join in a circle to begin working in the rnd, being very careful to untwist the knitting on the needles. P1, K9, P1, SM, then work 5 (6, 7, 8) reps of Row 15 of the Snowdrift Blanket chart as established.
Rnds 16-109: P1, K9, P1, SM then work 5, (6, 7, 8) reps of the corresponding row of the Snowdrift Blanket chart.
Work 1 (2, 2, 3) more reps of Rows 14-109 of the Snowdrift Blanket chart. Work 1 (0, 1, 0) more reps of Rows 14-61.
Work Rows 14-22 of Snowdrift Blanket chart once to create a final color border.

Top Border (worked flat)
Begin working flat (back and forth) with MC. Turn to WS.
Decrease Row (WS): P1 (1, 2, 2), *P2tog P3; rep from * 36 (43, 50, 57) times, P0 (1, 1, 2), BO last 11 sts. 145 (174, 203, 232) sts.

Rep Rows 1-12 of Bottom Border Seed stitch, then BO loosely in pattern.

Steeks
Reinforcement Method 1 – Sewing Machine: Using a sewing machine and long straight stitch, sew two vertical lines between adjacent sts on either side of the midline of the steek. The two sewn lines should be about 1" apart. Be careful to keep the line of machine stitching between the same two columns of sts all the way down.

Reinforcement Method 2 – by Hand: Using a crochet hook and MC, and working from bottom to top, create a vertical slip stitch column in the 3rd K st from the left of the steek. Start by inserting the hook from front to back of the middle of the st on the first row of the steek and pulling up a loop. *Insert the hook through the next vertical st and pull up a loop of the long end of the yarn and tighten. Rep from * until the last row of the steek is reached then tie off. Create a second vertical slip stitch column in the 7th K st from the left of the steek.

Once the steek is reinforced it can be cut. Cut the steek vertically in the middle of the 5th K st of the steek, at the midpoint between the two reinforced stitch columns.

Side Borders
Right Border
PM on the first colorwork st of Row 13 (at the end of the bottom seed st border), and repeats on Row 61, 109, 157, 207, 253, etc. With the crochet hook, the circular needle, and MC, starting at the bottom right edge, draw up a loop through the first (left-most) P st of the steek and slip it onto the needle. Rep for the next two rows, then skip a row. Cont picking up sts on 3 consecutive rows, then skipping the 4th row until sts are picked up along the entire edge and there are 201 (236, 271, 306) sts on the needle. Additionally, use the M and the table below to double check the balance of the number of picked up sts, and adjust as necessary to achieve 201, (236, 271, 306) sts.

Bottom Seed st border	Motif #1	Motif #2	Motif #3	Motif #4	Motif #5
9	35	35	35	35	35

Motif #6 (M, L, X-L)	Motif #7 (L, X-L)	Motif #8 (X-L)	Last colorwork border	Top Seed st border
35	35	35	8	9

Row 1: *K1, P1; rep from * across.
Row 2: K the P sts, and P the K sts..
Rows 3-12: Rep Rows 1-2 for a total of 12 rows of Seed stitch. BO in pattern.

Left Border
Follow instructions for Right Border, with this modification: start picking up sts at the top left corner of the blanket, and insert crochet hook into the RH P st of the steek.

Finishing

With MC, tack raw edge of steeks to the WS of the blanket and weave in yarn ends. Block blanket to measurements. Wash and tumble dry backing material and press. Mark the direction of the vertical nap of the fabric with fabric pencil or safety pins in several places.

Sizes Medium, Large and X-Large: Fold fabric width-wise so that cut edges are together. Cut along the resulting fold line. Rotate one of the pieces of fabric 180 degrees with respect to the other piece so that RSs are together and naps are in the same direction. On one selvedge edge, cut off selvedges from both pieces, and pin together edges along cut selvedges, matching patterns and sew together 5/8" from edge. Zig zag raw edges and press seam open. Resulting piece will be 88" by 54 (63, 72)".

Lay fabric on a large, flat surface, RS up. The fabric seam will be horizontal with respect to the blanket. Lay knitted blanket RS down over the fabric and adjust to center. Pin blanket to fabric around all edges. Being careful not to cut the blanket, cut the fabric 0.25" outside the blanket edge. Unpin the top and the bottom of the fabric and fold back fabric 2" or the amount needed to expose all of the seed stitch hems. Fold this edge under again 1" in from the edge and finger press and pin all folds.

On the right and left side of the blanket on the knitted/blanket side, add pins 1.5" in from the outside edge. Using a sewing machine and a long stitch or hand sewing, and thread matching MC, sew the backing to the blanket. Trim the fabric to 5/8" and zig zag the edges to secure.

Turn the blanket and backing RS out. Whip stitch the ends shut.

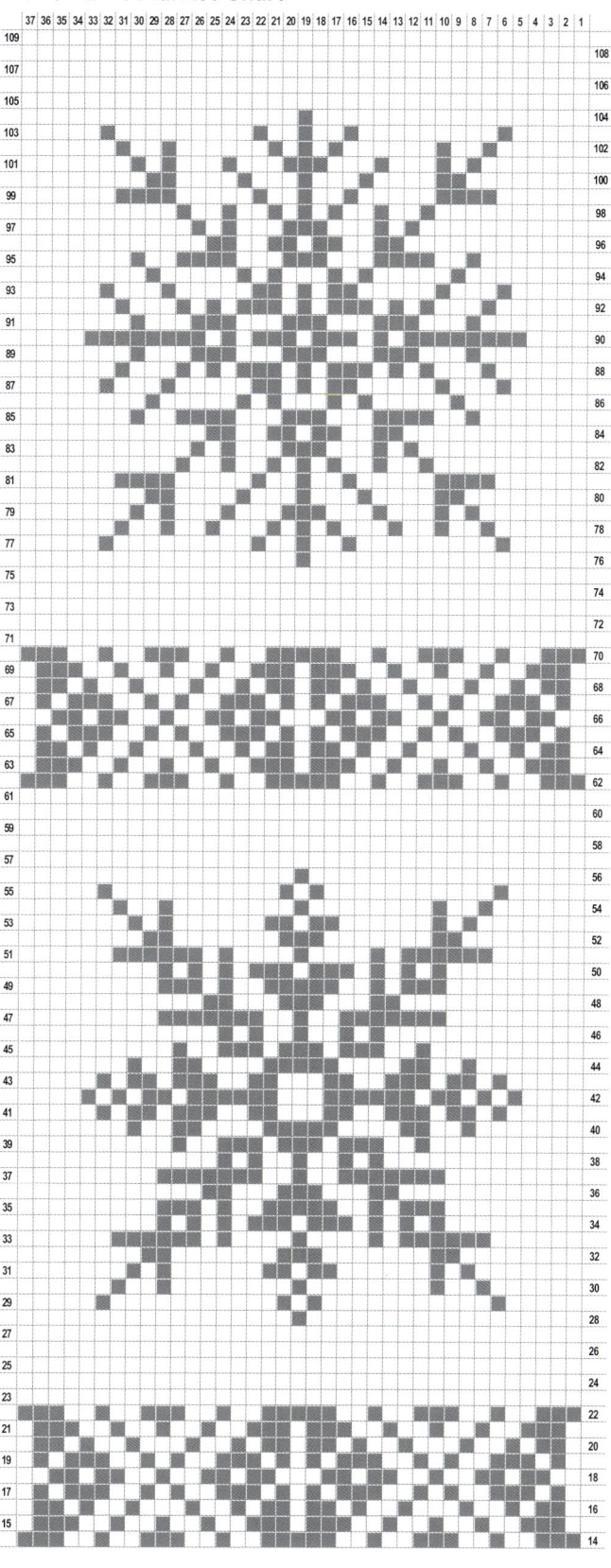

Legend:

☐ **knit**
RS: knit stitch
WS: purl stitch

☐ MC

■ C1

Snowdrift Blanket 21

HOLIDAY STOCKINGS
by Michele Lee Bernstein

FINISHED MEASUREMENTS
2 stockings, 19" long x 8" wide

YARN
Knit Picks Wool of the Andes Superwash Bulky (100% Superwash Wool; 137 yards/100g): Garnet Heather 26507, Solstice Heather 26521, White 26522; 1 hank each

NEEDLES
US 9 (5.5mm) 16" circular needle and DPNs, or size to obtain gauge

NOTIONS
Yarn Needle
Stitch Markers

GAUGE
16 sts and 18 rnds = 4" in Speckles Stitch Pattern in the round, blocked

For pattern support, pdxknitterati@comcast.net

Holiday Stockings

Notes:
These festive oversized holiday stockings are knit in the round from the cuff down to the toe, with a heel flap that is worked flat. A choice of two cuff motifs in stranded colorwork allows you to choose your own adventure. The Speckles Stitch Pattern adds interest to the leg, leading to a shallow heel and star toe. A separately knit I-cord hanging loop completes the stocking. Gauge is not critical, but a relatively firm fabric will help support the treats you place in your stocking.

If you wish to make two stockings as shown using 1 skein of each of 3 colors, knit the Reindeer Stocking first. You will use almost all of the color that is used for the reindeer motif and the body of the second stocking. Begin each stocking with 6 rnds of K2, P2 Ribbing instead of 8, and if necessary reduce the number of rows on the foot of the second stocking by 4.

Read each chart row from right to left as a RS row, repeating it twice across the round. C1 is always White. Choose which colors will be MC and C2 (motif color) before beginning.

K2, P2 Ribbing (in the rnd over multiples of 4 sts)
All Rnds: *K2, P2; rep from * to end.

Speckles Stitch Pattern (in the rnd over multiples of 4 sts)
Rnd 1: K1 in MC, *K1 in C1, K3 in MC; rep from * to last 3 sts, K1 in C1, K2 in MC.
Rnds 2, 3, 4: K with MC.
Rnd 5: *K3 in MC, K1 in C1; rep from * to end of rnd.
Rnds 6, 7, 8: K with MC.
Rep Rnds 1-8 for pattern.

Managing 2 Color Stranded Knitting
Carrying an unused color yarn for more than 1" (about 5 sts) can leave an undesirably long "float" on the back of the work that is easily snagged. To avoid this, loosely twist the working yarn and the carried yarn around each other to avoid floats longer than 5 sts. It is easiest to hide the twist above a st of the carried color in the previous rnd. This is especially helpful in the Reindeer chart.

DIRECTIONS
Using circular needle and MC, CO 64 sts. PM and join to work in the rnd, being careful not to twist. Work K2, P2 Ribbing for 8 rnds.

Cuff Motif
Work your choice of Snowflake chart or Reindeer chart, using MC for first two rnds, and C1 for background and C2 for motif. After completing chart, cut C2, leaving 8" tail.

Leg
Rnds 1-30: Work Speckles Stitch Pattern with MC and C1.
Rnd 31: Work Pattern Rnd 7, leaving last 16 sts of rnd unworked. Cut MC, leaving 8" tail.

Heel
Heel Flap
All slipped sts at beginning of rows are slipped P-wise in this section. Using C1, K 32 sts. These are last 16 sts of unfinished rnd, and 16 sts of next rnd. Heel will be worked back on forth on these 32 sts.
Row 1 (WS): Sl 1, P31, turn.
Row 2 (RS): Sl 1, K31, turn.
Rep Rows 1-2 five more times.
Next Row: Sl 1, P31, turn.

Turn Heel
Row 1: Sl 1, K17, SSK, K1, turn. 1 st dec.
Row 2: Sl 1, P5, P2tog, P1, turn. 1 st dec.
Row 3: Sl 1, K6, SSK, K1, turn. 1 st dec.
Row 4: Sl 1, P7, P2tog, P1, turn. 1 st dec.
Cont in this manner, working 1 more st before the dec in each row until all sts have been worked, ending with a WS row. You will not have enough sts to work last K1 or P1 on last 2 rows. 18 sts.
K 9 sts, ending at center heel, PM. Do not cut yarn.

Foot
Sts that are picked up and knit in this section are picked up TBL for added strength.
Set-up Rnd: Using MC, K9 (second half of heel), PU & K 7 sts along left side of heel flap, PU & K 1 st between heel flap and instep, K 32 instep sts, PU & K 1 st between instep and heel flap, PU & K 7 sts along right side of heel flap, K9 heel sts (to marker). 66 sts on needle, and you are ready to work Rnd 1 of Speckles Stitch Pattern.
Next Rnd: Dec the extra st between heel and instep away while maintaining Speckles Pattern (K2tog with last heel st on left side of heel, and SSK with first st on right side of heel).
Cont in Speckles Pattern on remaining 64 sts for 15 rnds total, ending with Pattern Rnd 7. Cut MC, leaving 8" tail.

Star Toe
Rnd 1: Using C1, K 1 rnd.
Rnd 2: *K9, K2tog, K19, K2tog; rep from * once more. 4 sts dec. 60 sts.
Rnd 3 and all odd rnds through 13: K all sts.
Rnd 4: *K8, K2tog; rep from * to end of rnd. 6 sts dec. 54 sts.
Rnd 6: *K7, K2tog; rep from * to end of rnd. 6 sts dec. 48 sts.
Continue to alternate dec rnds and plain rnds, working 1 fewer st before dec, through Rnd 13, changing to DPNs on Rnd 8.
Rnd 14: *K3, K2tog; rep from * to end of rnd. 24 sts.
Rnd 15: *K2, K2tog; rep from * to end of rnd. 18 sts.
Rnd 16: *K1, K2tog; rep from * to end of rnd. 12 sts.
Rnd 17: *K2tog; rep from * to end of rnd. 6 sts.
Cut yarn, leaving 8" tail. Thread tail through remaining sts and draw up snugly. Fasten off.

Finishing
I-Cord Hanging Loop
Using 2 DPNs and MC, CO 4 sts. K4. *Slide sts back to other end of DPN, bring yarn around snugly and K4. Rep from * until cord measures 6". Cut yarn, leaving 10" tail. Run yarn through sts and pull tight.

Use ends of I-cord to sew hanging loop to inside of center back of stocking below ribbing. Weave in all ends. Lightly steam block.

Reindeer Chart

Snowflake Chart

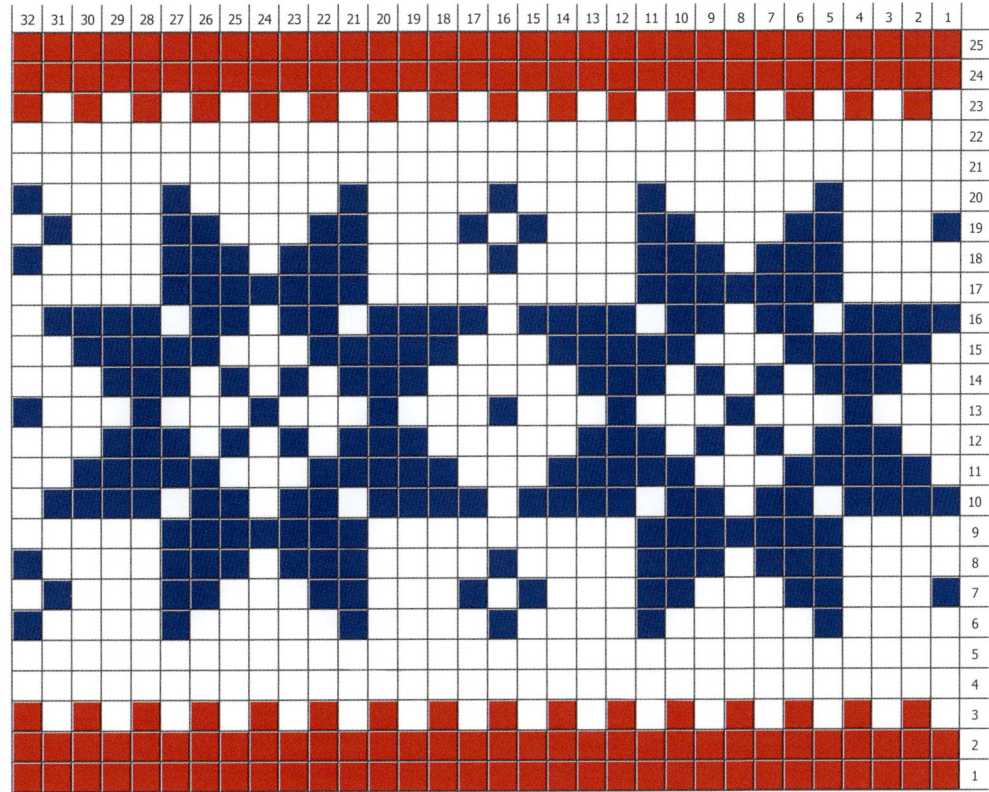

Legend:
- ☐ **knit** knit stitch
- ☐ C1
- 🟥 MC (snowflake chart) or C2 (reindeer chart)
- 🟦 MC (reindeer chart) or C2 (snowflake chart)

Holiday Stockings 25

NORDIC STAR PILLOW

by Margaret Mills

FINISHED MEASUREMENTS
17" Square

YARN
Knit Picks Wool of the Andes (100% Peruvian Highland Wool; 110 yards/50g): MC Larch Heather 25989, 3 balls; C1 White 24065, 2 balls

Knit Picks Shadow Lace (100% Merino Wool; 440 yards/50g): C2 Larch Heather 25921, 1 hank

NEEDLES
US 5 (3.75mm) straight or circular needles, or size to obtain gauge
US 7 (4.5mm) straight or circular needles plus DPN's for I-cord, or size to obtain gauge

NOTIONS
Yarn Needle
Stitch Markers
Scrap Yarn or Stitch Holder
Small Crochet Hook (optional)
3 Buttons
16" Pillow Form

GAUGE
Worsted yarn: 20 sts and 26 rows = 4" in St st on larger needles, blocked.
Worsted yarn: 20 sts and 40 rows = 4" in Garter stitch on smaller needles, blocked.
Lace yarn: 16 sts and 30 rows = 4" in St st on larger needles, firmly blocked.
Lace yarn: 14 sts and 24 rows = 4" over openwork portions of lace chart on larger needles, firmly blocked.

For pattern support, contact margaretgracemills@gmail.com

Nordic Star Pillow

Notes:

Whether you'd like to try out Estonian lace without committing to a whole shawl, or have a way to display your lace-knitting chops, this pillow has you covered. Unlike in a shawl, the lace fabric stays stretched out over the pillow form and the design remains visible! The effect of nupps lining the openwork trapezoids in this Nordic Star design is reminiscent of fabric cutouts popular in high fashion right now.

The pillow cover is knit in a combination of worsted weight and lace weight yarns, in one long piece, then assembled and finished – all without seaming! First, in the worsted MC: a garter stitch button band in the middle of the back, stockinette to the lower edge of the pillow, and a garter stitch turning row. Second, in the worsted C1: stockinette for the under-layer front of the pillow. Third, in the lace weight: the over-layer panel picked up from the MC turning row. Fourth, in the worsted MC: knit together the worsted under-layer and lace over-layer, a garter stitch turning row, stockinette to the middle of the back, and a garter stitch buttonhole band. After blocking, the final steps! Fifth, in the worsted MC: with the worsted MC portions of the pillow cover folded into place, pick up and knit through all layers of the cover along each side. Sixth (and finally), in the worsted MC: work applied I-cord around the entire edge of the pillow. Sew on some buttons, finish your ends, and it's finished!

The gauge for the lace fabric is much looser than that for the stockinette fabric in lace yarn, so extra stitches and extra rows are worked in the stockinette sections. When working short rows around the nupps, the line of nupps gets distorted if you wrap the stitch before the nupp rather than wrapping the nupp itself. To wrap a nupp in progress: slip all 7 loops to the RH needle, wrap the yarn around them, then slip all 7 loops back to the LH needle. On the next WS row, P the wrap together with the 7 loops in the nupp. When working the chart, follow RS rows (odd numbers) from right to left, and WS rows (even numbers) from left to right.

Stockinette Stitch (St st, worked flat)
Row 1 (RS): Knit.
Row 2 (WS): Purl.
Rep Rows 1-2 for pattern.

A tutorial for the Backward Loop CO can be found here: http://tutorials.knitpicks.com/loop-cast-on/

A tutorial for the Cable Cast On can be found here: http://tutorials.knitpicks.com/cabled-cast-on/

One-Row Buttonhole
Sl next st P-wise, bring yarn between needles, * Sl next st P-wise, PSSO; rep from * 2 times. 3 sts BO. Turn work. Using Cable CO, CO 4 sts. Turn work. Sl next st P-wise, pass last CO st over.

DIRECTIONS

Lower Back
Button Band
Using MC and smaller needles, CO 83 sts. K 11 rows, ending with a WS row.

Next Row (RS): Switch to larger needles. Beginning with a K row, work in St st for 51 rows.
Next Row (WS, Turning Row): K.
Break MC, leaving a 3' tail.

Front Under-Layer
Using C1 and beginning with a RS row, work in St st for 106 rows, ending with a WS row.
Break C1. Put sts on a holder.

Front Over-Layer
With RS facing, turn piece upside down, so that C1 is below/toward you and MC is above/away from you.
Using C2 lace weight yarn and smaller needles, PU and K through the bottom loop of each st in the turning row. 83 sts. Turn so that C1 is above again.
Dec Row (RS): Switch to larger needles. K3, (K2tog, K3) to end. 67 sts.
Next Row (WS): Work in St st for 11 rows.
Next Row (RS): K11, PM, work Row 1 of Nordic Star Lace chart, PM, K11.
Work from Nordic Star Lace chart through Row 98, working short rows as indicated in the chart. Remove Markers.
Next Row (RS): Work in St st for 11 rows.
Inc Row (WS): P3, (M1, P4) to end. 83 sts. Break C2.

Upper Back
Return under-layer sts to needle. Using larger needles and MC, work across row, K2tog one over-layer st together with one under-layer st, joining the two layers together. 83 sts.
Next Row (WS, Turning Row): K.
Next Row (RS): Work in St st for 51 rows.

Buttonhole Band
Switch to smaller needles. K 5 rows.
Next Row (RS): K19, (work One-row Buttonhole, K18) 3 times, K1.
K 4 rows.
BO all sts. Break MC.

Finishing
Weave in ends of lace yarn but not MC or C1, wash and block flat to diagram.

I-cord Edging
Fold on turning rows and pin or baste sides in place, overlapping buttonhole band outside of button band.
Sides: For right side, use the MC strand left over from end of lower back. For left side, use MC from ball. Using smaller needles (and small crochet hook to help PU sts if desired) and MC, PU and K 83 sts along the right side of the pillow: pick up the outside leg of stitches in all three layers, picking up roughly 3 out of every 4 St st rows and 1 out of every 2 garter st rows (1 st per garter ridge).

Using DPNs, CO 4 sts using Backward Loop Cast On. Pick up 1 garter loop from turning row at bottom of pillow.
Work I-cord BO as follows: K3, SKP final stitch on DPN with garter loop. Pick up 1 garter loop from turning row at bottom of pillow. Slide sts back to other end of the DPN.
Repeat this row until all garter loops along bottom of pillow have been incorporated in I-cord BO.

First Corner: After final garter loop has been incorporated, work 1 row of plain I-cord, then work another row of I-cord BO into the same garter loop.

Work I-cord BO along right side, incorporating live sts, until corner.

Second Corner: Work one row I-cord BO into the first garter loop of the turning row at the top of the pillow, then one plain row of I-cord, then another row of I-cord BO into the same garter loop.

Work I-cord BO along top as for bottom, incorporating the garter loops from turning row. Work another corner in the final garter loop of the turning row.

Work I-cord BO along left side, incorporating live sts.

Next Row: Pick up first garter loop from turning row at bottom of pillow. K3, SKP final stitch on DPN with garter loop.

Break yarn. Graft live sts to start of I-cord.

Sew buttons to button band underneath buttonholes. Weave in all ends, insert pillow form.

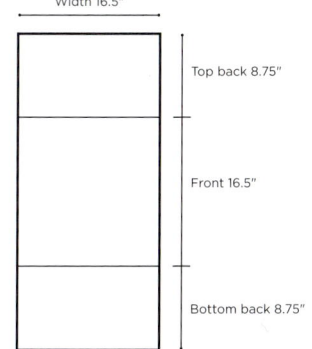

Width 16.5"
Top back 8.75"
Front 16.5"
Bottom back 8.75"

Legend:

☐ **knit**
RS: knit stitch
WS: purl stitch

⋀ **close nupp**
Purl seven stitches together as one

○ **yo**
yarn over

\ **ssk**
Slip one stitch as if to knit, Slip another stitch as if to knit. Insert left-hand needle into front of these 2 stitches and knit them together

/ **k2tog**
Knit two stitches together as one stitch

V **slip**
Slip stitch as if to purl, holding yarn in back

M **make one**
Make one by lifting strand in between stitch just worked and the next stitch, knit into back of this thread.

⊌ **nupp7**
In one st, KFB three times, K1. (Results in seven sts in one st.) Turn work, P these seven sts. Turn work, K the seven sts.

⊘ 7-stich nupp worked into 2 sts (K2tog)

⊘ 7-stich nupp worked into 2 sts (ssk)

φ Wrap and Turn

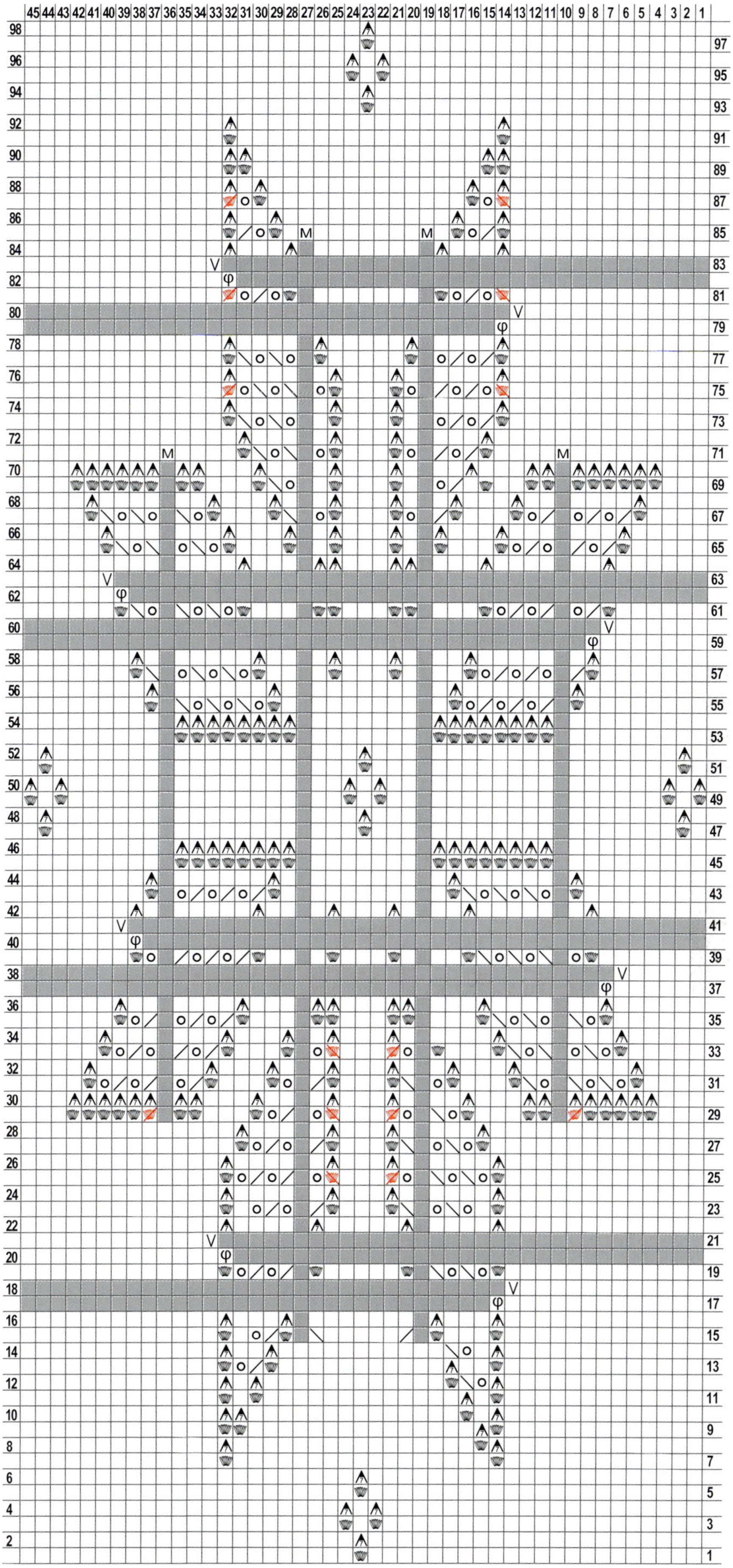

Nordic Star Pillow

TINY HEARTS

by Mone Dräger

FINISHED MEASUREMENTS
2.5" high x 2" wide at widest point

YARN
Knit Picks Palette (100% Peruvian Highland Wool; 231 yards/50g): Pimento 24246, White 23728, Turmeric 24251, 1 ball each

NEEDLES
US 1 (2.5mm) DPNs or two 24" circular needles for two circulars technique, or one 32" or longer circular needle for Magic Loop technique, or size to obtain gauge

NOTIONS
Yarn Needle
Scrap Yarn or Stitch Holder
Fiberfill

GAUGE
36 sts and 48 rows = 4" over stranded St st in the rnd, blocked.

Tiny Hearts

Notes:

The hearts are started with a Circular Cast On and are knitted from the bottom up. They are worked in the round; at the top the stitches are divided to continue with each of the heart arches individually. To finish these segments the final stitches are grafted together. The hearts are filled with a small amount of fiberfill, which is added from the top between the two heart arches. The hole is closed afterwards with the yarn tail from casting on for the second arch.

Weave in all yarn tails other than the one needed for closing the filling hole while the work is still in progress.

The small holiday themed motifs are worked on the front and the back. Please take note that the motifs start on different rounds of the Basic Instructions, and always refer to the particular chart. Read each chart row from right to left, as a RS row. Each row is repeated twice across the round.

Circular Cast On

Hold the working yarn between the first and middle finger of your left hand and wrap the yarn tail around your ring and pinky fingers, holding the yarn tail with your right hand. *Using your right hand, insert the point of your needle under the yarn across your ring and pinky finger. Pass the needle over the working yarn and draw a loop out from under the yarn you first slid your needle under. Now pass the needle over the working yarn and draw a loop up as in a yarn over. Rep from * until you have CO on the required number of sts. Because you need an even number of sts, you will need to CO the final st as a standard YO when you begin the first rnd of knitting.

Arrange the sts on your needles to begin knitting in the rnd. Tug on the yarn tail to draw the sts into a tight circle and begin knitting. A tutorial for the Circular Cast On can be found at: http://tutorials.knitpicks.com/circular-cast-on/

A tutorial for the Backward Loop CO can be found at: http://tutorials.knitpicks.com/loop-cast-on/

When working the lifted increases, use the color shown on the chart as your working yarn to produce the st to achieve the desired motif.

M1L (make 1 left): Use your left needle to pick up the st that is two sts below the st just worked. Knit this st TBL.

M1R (make 1 right): Insert your right needle into the st below the st on the left needle. Knit this st.

Kitchener Stitch (grafting)

With an equal number of sts on two needles, thread end of working yarn through yarn needle. Hold needles parallel with RS's facing and both needles pointing to the right. Perform Step 2 on the first front st, and then Step 4 on the first back st, and then continue with instructions below.

1. Pull yarn needle K-wise though front st and drop st from knitting needle.
2. Pull yarn needle P-wise through next front st, leave st on knitting needle.
3. Pull yarn needle P-wise through first back st and drop st from knitting needle.
4. Pull yarn needle K-wise through next back st, leave st on knitting needle.

Repeat Steps 1 – 4 until all sts have been grafted.

DIRECTIONS

Basic Instructions for all Hearts

Please refer to the charts to see in which round the motif is started. On that rnd, join your desired CC color, working the motif colors as shown on the chart.

Using the Circular Cast on Method, CO 6 sts with your desired MC. Arrange them on the needle(s) so half of the sts form the front and half of the sts form the back.

Rnd 1 and all odd numbered rows: Knit.
Rnd 2: *K1, M1L, K1, M1R, K1; rep from * once. 10 sts.
Rnd 4: *K1, M1L, K3, M1R, K1; rep from * once. 14 sts.
Rnd 6: *K1, M1L, K5, M1R, K1; rep from * once. 18 sts.
Rnd 8: *K1, M1L, K7, M1R, K1; rep from * once. 22 sts.
Rnd 10: *K1, M1L, K9, M1R, K1; rep from * once. 26 sts.
Rnd 12: *K1, M1L, K11, M1R, K1; rep from * once. 30 sts.
Rnd 14: *K1, M1L, K13, M1R, K1; rep from * once. 34 sts.
Rnd 16: *K1, M1L, K15, M1R, K1; rep from * once. 38 sts.
Rnds 17-24: Knit.

At this point the sts are divided to work the two heart arches individually. The first arch is worked over the first 10 sts and the last 9 sts of the rnd.

Arch 1

Rnd 1: K1, SSK, K7, using the Backward Loop Cast On method CO 3, Place the next 19 sts in between on a stitch holder or scrap yarn. K6, K2tog, K1. 20 sts.
Rnds 2-3: K.
Rnd 4: *K1, SSK, K4, K2tog, K1; rep from * once. 16 sts.
Rnd 5: *K1, SSK, K2, K2tog, K1; rep from * once. 12 sts.
Break the yarn and graft remaining sts together using Kitchener Stitch.

Arch 2

Return sts on hold to needle(s). The arch is worked from the middle: with the front side facing re-join the working yarn, leaving a tail of approximately 6".

Set-up: Make a slip knot and place it on the RH needle; use the Backward Loop Cast On method to CO 1 st, PM for beginning of rnd.
Rnd 1: Use the Backwards Loop Cast on CO 1 st, K6, K2tog, K2, SSK, K9. 20 sts.
Continue as for Arch 1 from Rnd 2.

Finishing

Fill the heart with fiberfill to the desired shape and density. Thread the yarn tail from the CO of the second arch onto a needle and use it to close the gap between the two arches. Use a contrast colored thread of approximately 3" to add a hanger to the heart; attaching it at the deepest point between the arches.

As an optional finishing touch, a contrast colored thread can be woven loosely around the outer edges of the ornament, and also form the hanger. Cut a strand in CC of approximately 16" and thread it onto your yarn needle. Starting at the deepest point between the arches and leaving a tail of approximately 1.5", start to border the heart by loosely weaving the thread through every other stitch at the outer border of the heart until you return to the starting point. Use the tail from where you started and the remaining yarn for the hanger.

Legend:

 **make one left**
Place a firm backward loop over the right needle, so that the yarn end goes towards the front

 make one right
Place a firm backward loop over the right needle, so that the yarn end goes towards the back

- knit / knit stitch
- MC
- CC
- no stitch

Bell Chart
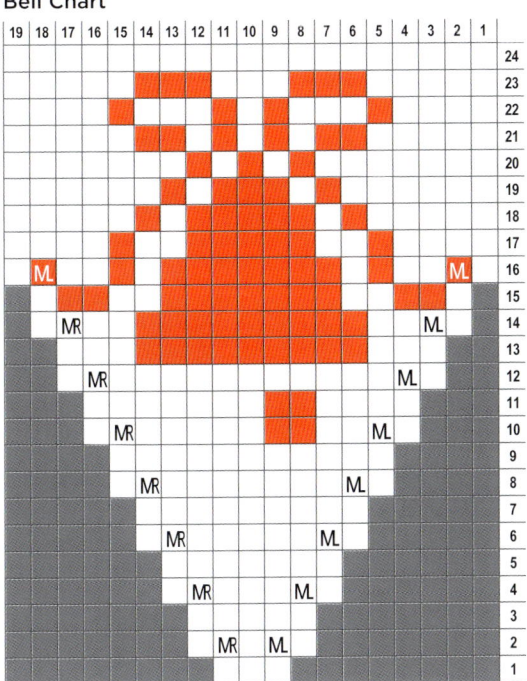

Reindeer Chart
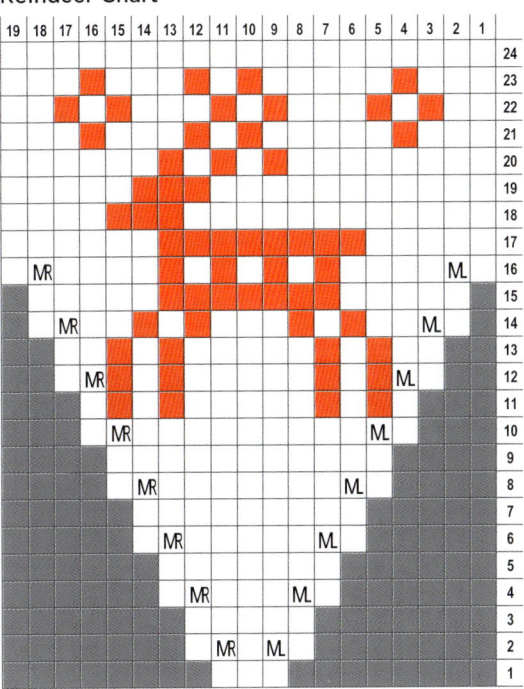

Christmas Tree Chart
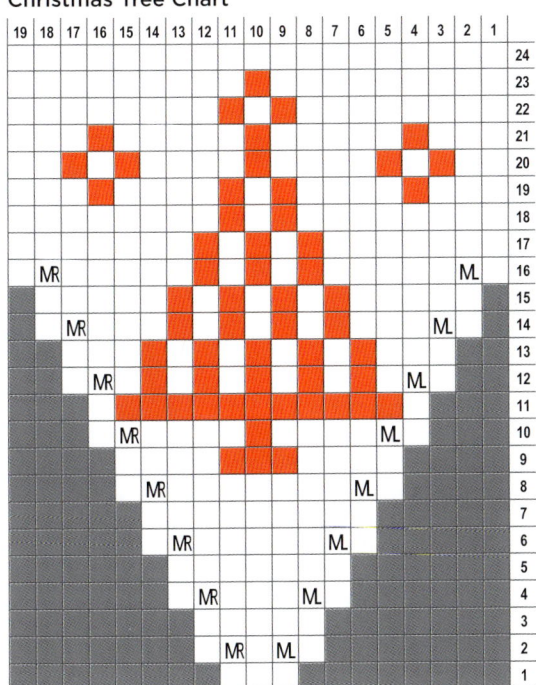

Couple Chart
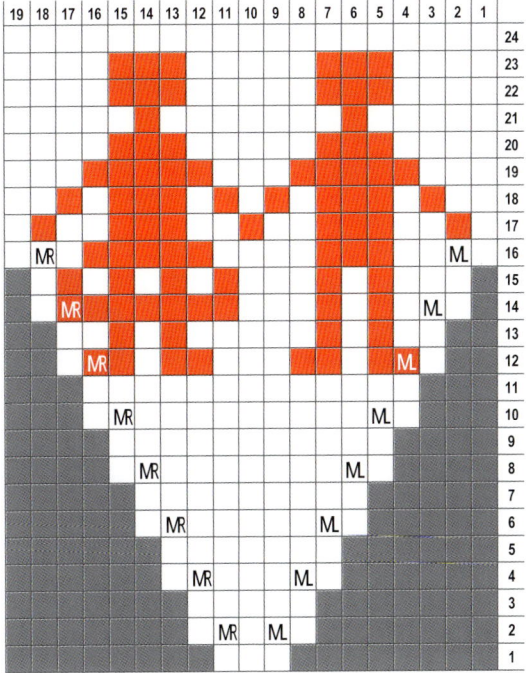

Tiny Hearts 33

Heart Chart

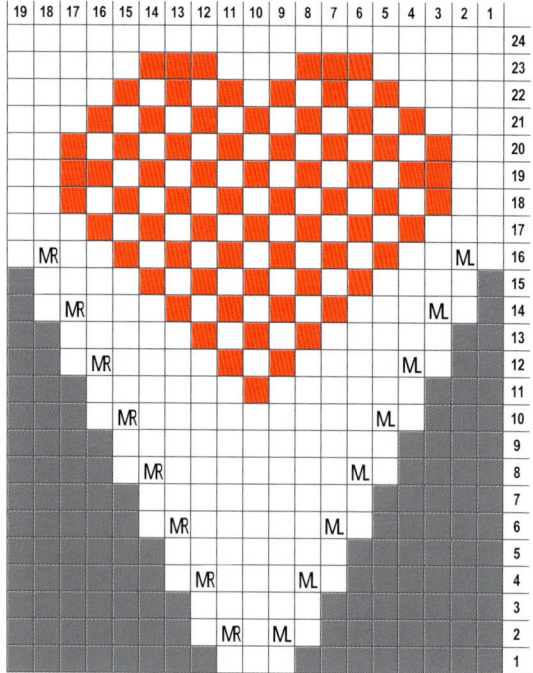

Snowman Chart

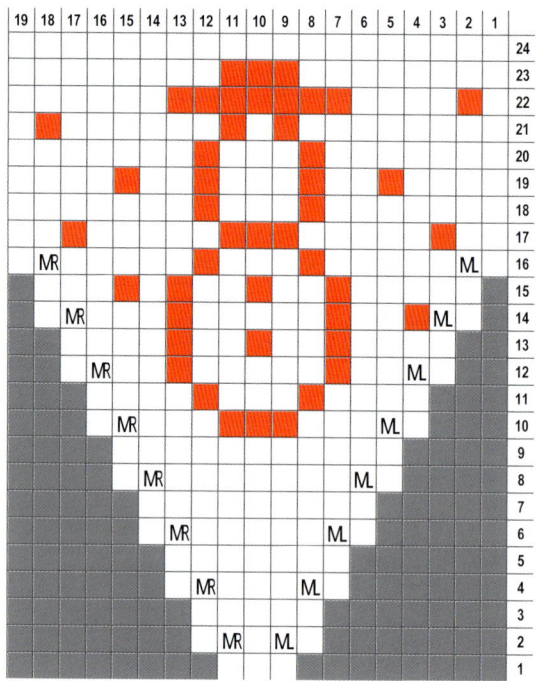

Snowflake Chart

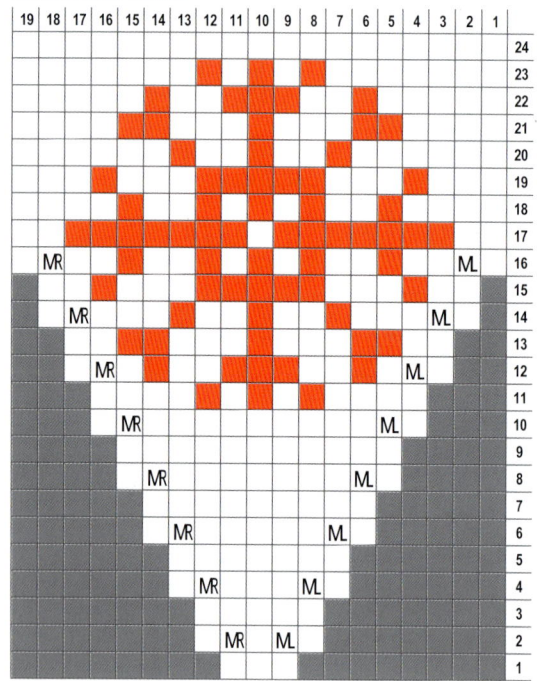

Star Chart

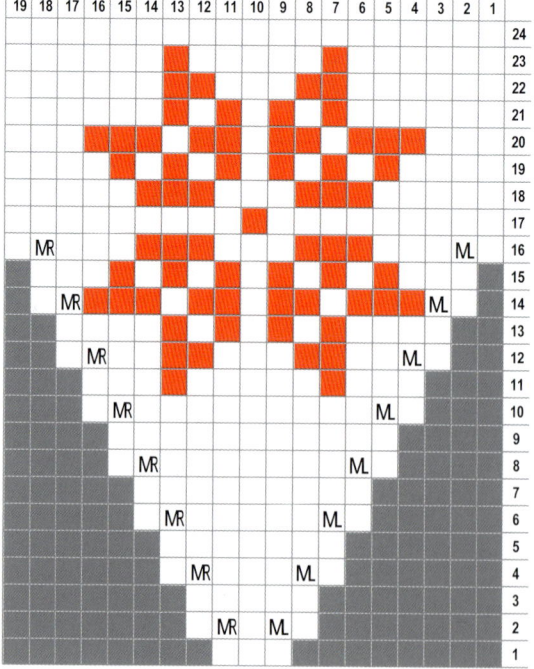

SNOWFLAKE BLANKET

by Quenna Lee

FINISHED MEASUREMENTS
31.5" x 40.5"

YARN
Knit Picks Swish Worsted (100% Superwash Merino; 110 yards/50g): Dove Heather 25631, 13 balls.

NEEDLES
US 8 (5mm) circular needles, or size to obtain gauge

NOTIONS
Yarn Needle
Stitch Markers

GAUGE
17 sts and 24 rows = 4" in St st and Moss Stitch Pattern, blocked.

Snowflake Blanket

Notes:
Snuggle up at home with this cozy lap blanket. A duo of snowflakes arranged in a checkerboard layout provides holiday cheer and visual interest. Moss stitch is used for the edging and around each snowflake square.

Charts are followed on RS rows from right to left, and on WS rows from left to right.

Moss Stitch Pattern (worked flat over an even number of sts)
Row 1 (RS): SL 1 st P-wise WYIF, (K1, P1) to last st, K1.
Row 2 (WS): Rep Row 1.
Row 3: SL 1 st P-wise WYIF, (P1, K1) to last st, K1.
Row 4: Rep Row 3.
Rep Rows 1-4 for pattern.

Chart A Pattern (worked flat over 17 sts)
Row 1: (RS): K.
Row 2 (WS): P.
Row 3: K.
Row 4: P8, K1, P8.
Row 5: K7, P3, K7.
Row 6: P3, K2, P3, K1, P3, K2, P3.
Row 7: K3, P2, K3, P1, K3, P2, K3.
Row 8: P5, (K1, P2) x 2, K1, P5.
Row 9: K6, (P1, K1) x 2, P1, K6.
Row 10: P2, K1, P4, K3, P4, K1, P2.
Row 11: K1, P15, K1.
Row 12: Rep Row 10.
Row 13: Rep Row 9.
Row 14: Rep Row 8.
Row 15: Rep Row 7.
Row 16: Rep Row 6.
Row 17: Rep Row 5.
Row 18: Rep Row 4.
Row 19: K.
Row 20: P.

Chart B Pattern (worked flat over 17 sts)
Row 1 (RS): K.
Row 2 (WS): P.
Rows 3 - 4: Rep Rows 1 - 2.
Row 5: (K5, P1) x 2, K5.
Row 6: P5, K2, P3, K2, P5.
Row 7: K5, P3, K1, P3, K5.
Row 8: P2, K3, (P1, K2) x 2, P1, K3, P2.
Row 9: K3, P3, (K1, P1) x 2, K1, P3, K3.
Row 10: P4, K3, P1, K1, P1, K3, P4.
Row 11: K7, P1, K1, P1, K7.
Row 12: Rep Row 10.
Row 13: Rep Row 9.
Row 14: Rep Row 8.
Row 15: Rep Row 7.
Row 16: Rep Row 6.
Row 17: Rep Row 5.
Row 18: P.
Row 19: K.
Row 20: P.

DIRECTIONS

Edging
CO 134 sts.
Rows 1-8: Work Moss Stitch Pattern.

Body
Row 1 (RS): Cont in pattern for 6 sts, PM, *(work Chart A, PM, cont in pattern for 4 sts, PM, work Chart B, PM, cont in pattern for 4 sts, PM); rep from * once; work Chart A, PM, cont in pattern for 4 sts, PM, work Chart B, PM, cont last 6 sts in pattern.

Rows 2-20: Cont in pattern until Rows 1-20 of Charts A and B have been completed.

Rows 21-26: Cont Moss Stitch Pattern to end.

Row 27 (RS): Cont in pattern to M, SM, *(work Chart B, SM, cont in pattern to M, SM, work Chart A, SM, cont in pattern to M, SM); rep from * once; work Chart B, cont in pattern to M, SM, work Chart A, SM, cont in pattern to end.

Rows 28-46: Cont in pattern until Rows 1-20 of Charts A and B have been completed.

Rows 47-52: Rep Rows 21-26.

Rows 53-208: Rep Rows 1-52 three more times.

Rows 209-228: Rep Rows 1-20 once.

Edging
Rows 1-7: Cont Moss Stitch Pattern to end.
Row 8 (WS): BO in pattern.

Finishing
Weave in ends, wash and block to measurements.

Snowflake Chart Diagram

B	A	B	A	B	A
A	B	A	B	A	B
B	A	B	A	B	A
A	B	A	B	A	B
B	A	B	A	B	A
A	B	A	B	A	B
B	A	B	A	B	A
A	B	A	B	A	B
B	A	B	A	B	A

Moss

Legend:

knit
RS: knit stitch
WS: purl stitch

● RS: purl stitch
WS: knit stitch

slip wyif
V Slip stitch as if to purl, with yarn in front

repeat pattern

Chart A

	17	16	15	14	13	12	11	10	9	8	7	6	5	4	3	2	1	
20																		
																		19
18									●									
								●	●	●								17
16				●	●				●				●	●				
				●	●				●				●	●				15
14						●			●			●						
							●		●		●							13
12			●				●	●	●					●				
	●	●	●	●	●	●	●	●	●	●	●	●	●	●	●			11
10			●				●	●	●					●				
							●		●		●							9
8						●			●			●						
				●	●				●				●	●				7
6				●	●				●				●	●				
							●	●	●									5
4									●									
																		3
2																		
																		1

Chart B

	17	16	15	14	13	12	11	10	9	8	7	6	5	4	3	2	1	
20																		
																		19
18																		
						●						●						17
16						●	●				●	●						
							●	●		●	●							15
14				●	●	●		●	●	●			●	●	●			
					●	●	●		●		●	●	●					13
12						●	●				●	●						
								●		●								11
10						●	●				●	●						
					●	●	●		●		●	●	●					9
8				●	●	●		●	●	●			●	●	●			
						●	●	●		●	●							7
6						●	●				●	●						
						●						●						5
4																		
																		3
2																		
																		1

TOWNSCAPE PILLOW

by Margaret Holzmann

FINISHED MEASUREMENTS
20" square

YARN
Knit Picks Mighty Stitch Worsted (80% Acrylic, 20% Superwash Wool; 208 yards/100g): C1 Spruce 26826, MC Cream 26831, 2 balls each

NEEDLES
US 7 (4.5mm) 24" circular needles, or size to obtain gauge

NOTIONS
Sewing Machine or Sewing Needle and E-4 (3.5 mm) Crochet Hook
Sewing Pins
Yarn Needle
3 Stitch Markers
White polyester blend Sewing Thread
16" All-purpose Zipper
20" Pillow Form

GAUGE
18.75 sts and 19.75 rows = 4" in stranded St st in the rnd, blocked

Townscape Pillow

Notes:
This pillow is worked in the round and uses a 'knitted steek;' a column of ten extra stitches which is reinforced after the pillow face is knitted, cut, folded to the inside of the pillow, and used as a facing for the zipper.

Each row of the chart is read from right to left, as a RS row. Knit, making color changes as indicated

DIRECTIONS
Pillow Body
With MC, CO 196 sts. PM before first st to mark beginning of rnd, after 10th st to mark end of steeks sts, and after 103rd st to mark end of first chart rep. Join to work in the rnd, being careful not to twist sts.

Rnds 1-99: SM, P1, K8, P1, *SM, work corresponding row of the Townscape Pillow chart; rep from * to end of rnd.

BO K-wise, leaving a 28" tail of MC for sewing the top seam.

Steeks

Reinforcement Method 1 – Sewing Machine: Using a sewing machine and long straight stitch, sew two vertical lines between adjacent sts on either side of the midline of the steek. The two sewn lines should be about 1" apart. Be careful to keep the line of machine stitching between the same two columns of sts all the way down.

Reinforcement Method 2 – by Hand: Using the crochet hook and MC, and working from bottom to top, create a vertical slip stitch column in the 3rd K st from the left of the steek. Start by inserting the hook from front to back of the middle of the st on the first row of the steek and pulling up a loop. *Insert the hook through the next vertical st and pull up a loop of the long end of the yarn and tighten. Rep from * until the last row of the steek is reached then tie off. Create a second vertical slip stitch column in the 6th K st from the left of the steek.

Once the steek is reinforced it can be cut. Cut the steek vertically between the 4th and 5th K sts of the steek, at the midpoint between the two reinforced stitch columns.

Finishing
Block to measurements if desired, although the pillow form will tend to stretch the knitting to the desired measurements, and weave in ends. Open the zipper completely. Lay the RS of the zipper face down on the RS of the left selvedge edge of the pillow face. Adjust vertically to center the zipper along the edge. Place zipper so that the center line of sewing will be over the purl st of the steek. Pin in place. Hand baste right side of zipper then machine stitch, or hand sew zipper using a backstitch. Close zipper. Turn pillow cover inside out. Align left side of zipper top and bottom with RS of the right selvedge edge of the pillow face and pin. Open zipper and turn pillow cover RS out and continue pinning in place. Hand baste left side of zipper to right pillow selvedge edge then machine stitch, or hand sew zipper using a back stitch.

Using 28" yarn tail and a whip stitch, close the pillow cover and side seam, ending at the top of the zipper and tying off securely. Using another 28" of MC, and starting at the lower left corner of the pillow cover, use a whip stitch to close the pillow cover and right side seam, ending at the bottom of the zipper, and tie off securely.

Townscape Pillow

Legend:

☐ **knit**
RS: knit stitch
WS: purl stitch

☐ MC

▨ C1

TANNENBAUM TREE SKIRT
by Allison Griffith

FINISHED MEASUREMENTS
12" depth x 27" in diameter, approximate

YARN
Knit Picks Brava Bulky (100% Premium Acrylic; 136 yards/100g): Cream 25725, 4 balls

NEEDLES
US 10 (6mm) 40" or longer circular needles, or size to obtain gauge

NOTIONS
Yarn Needle
Stitch Markers
Cable Needle

GAUGE
13 sts and 22 rows = 4" in Garter Stitch, blocked. Gauge for this project is approximate

Tannenbaum Tree Skirt

Notes:
This small tree skirt is worked flat, from the outside edge toward the center. The cables are fully charted, so be sure to carefully read the chart as you work. RS rows are odd-numbered and read from right to left. WS rows are even-numbered and read from left to right.

DIRECTIONS

CO as follows, placing markers as you go: CO 4, PM (CO 29, PM, CO 3, PM) 8 times, CO 1. 261 sts.

Work Tannenbaum Chart Rows 1-65, repeating the section highlighted in red 8 times each row. Stitch markers should align with the outside of the vertical 2x2 cables.

BO after Row 65.

Finishing
Weave in ends, wash and block to measurements.

Legend:

- **knit**
  RS: knit stitch
  WS: purl stitch
- **purl**
  RS: purl stitch
  WS: knit stitch
- **make one**
  Make one by lifting strand in between stitch just worked and the next stitch, knit into back of this thread
- **p2tog**
  RS: Purl 2 stitches together
  WS: Knit 2 stitches together
- **k2tog**
  RS: Knit two stitches together
  WS: Purl 2 stitches together
- **p3tog**
  RS: Purl three stitches together
  WS: Knit three stitches together as one
- **repeat**
- **no stitch**

- **c2 over 1 right**
  sl2 to CN, hold in front. k1, k2 from CN
- **c2 over 1 left**
  sl1 to CN, hold in back. k2, k1 from CN
- **c2 over 2 right**
  sl2 to CN, hold in back. k2, k2 from CN
- **c2 over 2 left**
  sl 2 to CN, hold in front. k2, k2 from CN
- **c2 over 3 right**
  sl3 to CN, hold in back. k2, then k3 from CN
- **c2 over 3 left**
  sl2 to CN, hold in front. k3, k2 from CN
- **c3 over 3 right split**
  sl3 to CN, hold in back. k2, k1 from CN, hold CN in front, k1, k2 from CN
- **c4 over 2 right split**
  sl4 to CN, hold in back. k2, sl last 2 sts from CN to LH needle, bring CN in front, k2 from LH needle, k2 from CN

Tannenbaum Chart

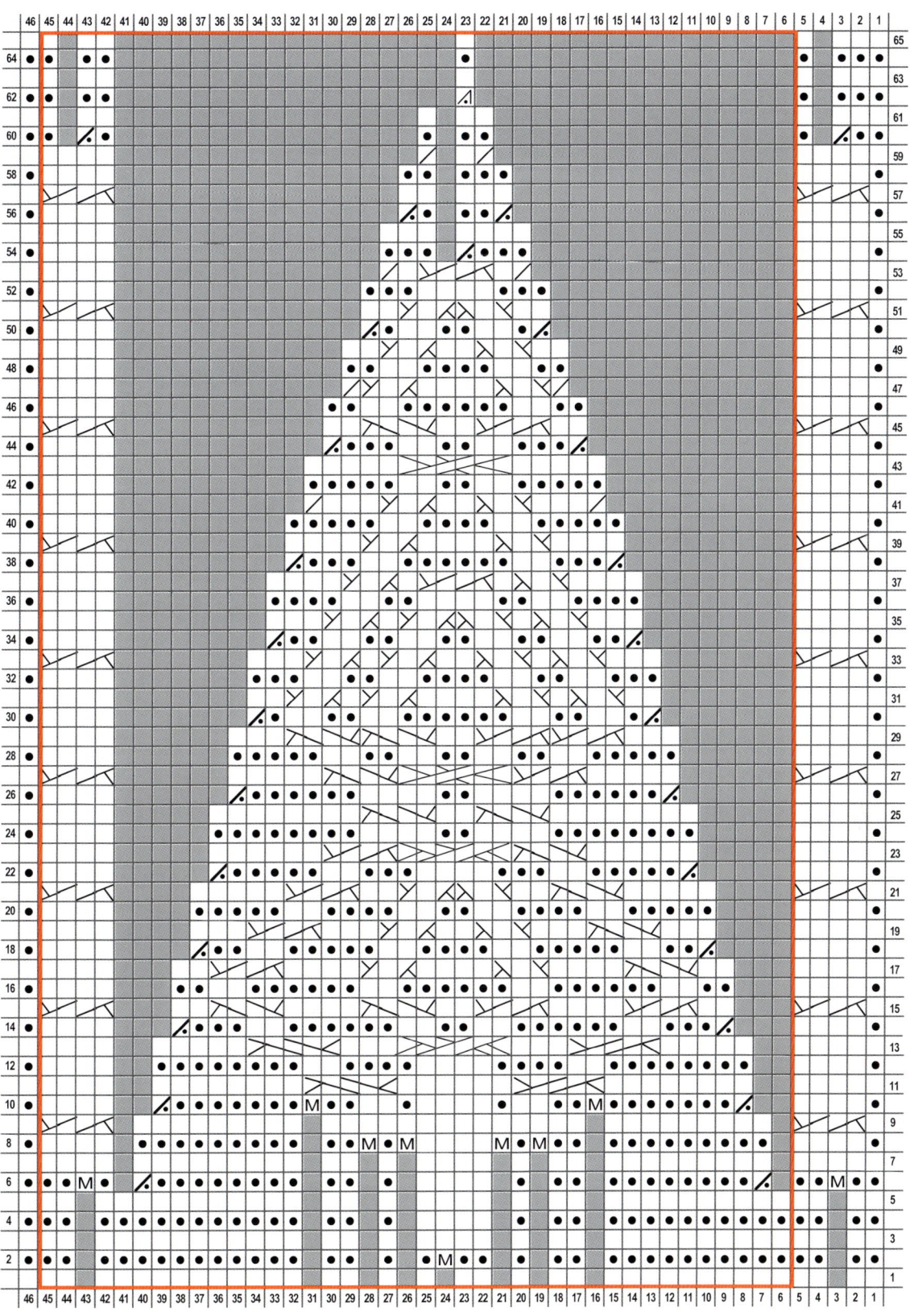

Tannnenbaum Tree Skirt 47

FESTIVE FAIR ISLE ORNAMENTS

by Emily Kintigh

FINISHED MEASUREMENTS
10" circumference x 3.5" tall, not including hanging loop

YARN
Knit Picks Stroll Sock Yarn (75% Superwash Merino Wool, 25% Nylon; 231 yards/50g): MC Firecracker Heather 24587, C1 White 26082, 1 ball each

NEEDLES
US 1 (2.25mm) two 24" circular needles for two circulars technique, or one 32" or longer circular needle for Magic Loop technique, plus two DPNs, or size to obtain gauge

NOTIONS
Yarn Needle
Stitch Markers
Stuffing

GAUGE
37 sts and 48 rows = 4" in stranded St st in the round

Festive Fair Isle Ornaments

Notes:

The ornaments are worked in the round from the bottom up and stuffed before finishing. The increases and decreases are the same for each ornament. There are four options for the design in the middle. All charts are repeated four times across the rnd, read each chart row from right to left.

The ornaments take a small amount of yarn. One ball in each color is more than enough to make the set of four. It is enough to make about seven ornaments.

M1L (Make 1 Left-leaning stitch): PU the bar between st just worked and next st and place on LH needle as a regular stitch; K TBL.

M1R (Make 1 Right-leaning stitch): PU the bar between st just worked and next st and place on LH needle backwards (incorrect stitch mount). K through the front loop.

I-Cord

All Rows: K to end. Slide sts from left end of needle to the right bringing the yarn behind the work and pulling snuggly, creating a tube.

DIRECTIONS

Ornaments

With MC, CO 8 sts. PM and join in the rnd being careful not to twist the sts.

Rnd 1: K to end.

Rnd 2: KFB to end. 16 sts.

Work Increases Chart across all sts. 72 sts.

Work the Snowflake Chart, Reindeer Chart, Tree Chart, or Bird Chart (depending on which ornament is being made) across all sts. Weave in CO end and tail from joining C1.

Work Decreases Chart across all sts, cutting and weaving in end from C1 then adding stuffing after Rnd 15 of chart. Add more stuffing after Rnd 19 if needed. 4 sts.

Loop

Transfer remaining sts to a DPN. Work an I-Cord for 4". BO all sts.

Finishing

Sew BO end of I-Cord to top of ornament to form a loop. Weave in end.

Legend:
- knit — knit stitch
- no stitch
- MC
- C1
- ssk — Slip one stitch as if to knit, Slip another stitch as if to knit. Insert left-hand needle into front of these 2 stitches and knit them together
- k2tog — Knit two stitches together as one stitch
- ML — make one left — Place a firm backward loop over the right needle, so that the yarn end goes towards the front
- MR — make one right — Place a firm backward loop over the right needle, so that the yarn end goes towards the back

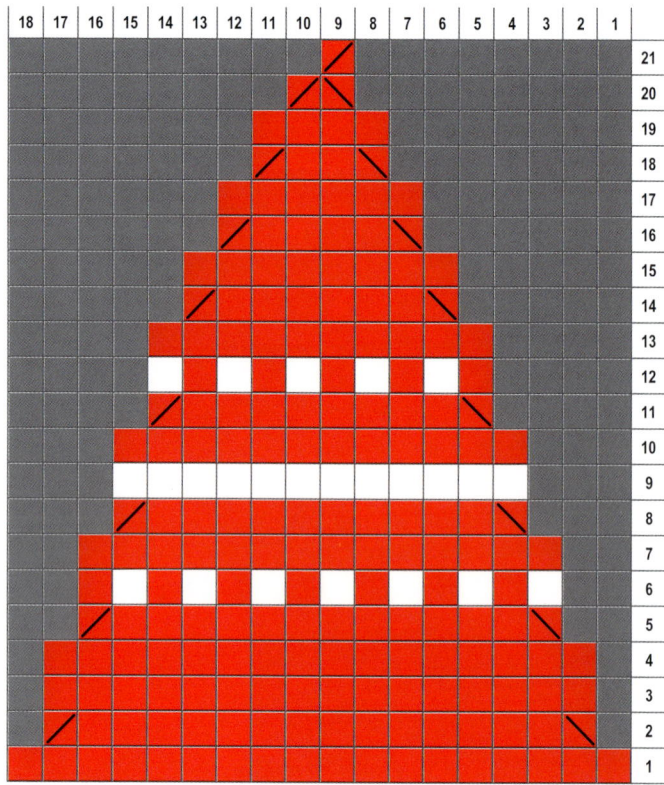

Decreases Chart

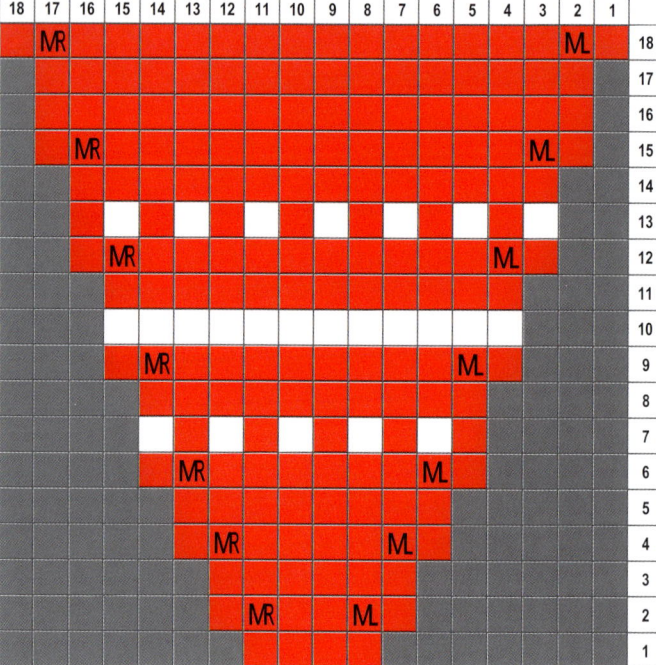

Increases Chart

Bird Chart

Reindeer Chart

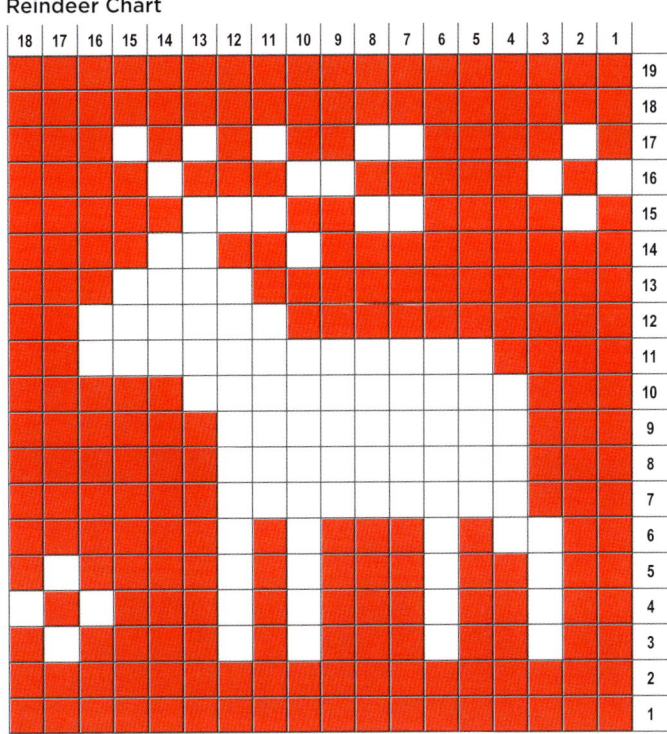

Snowflake Chart

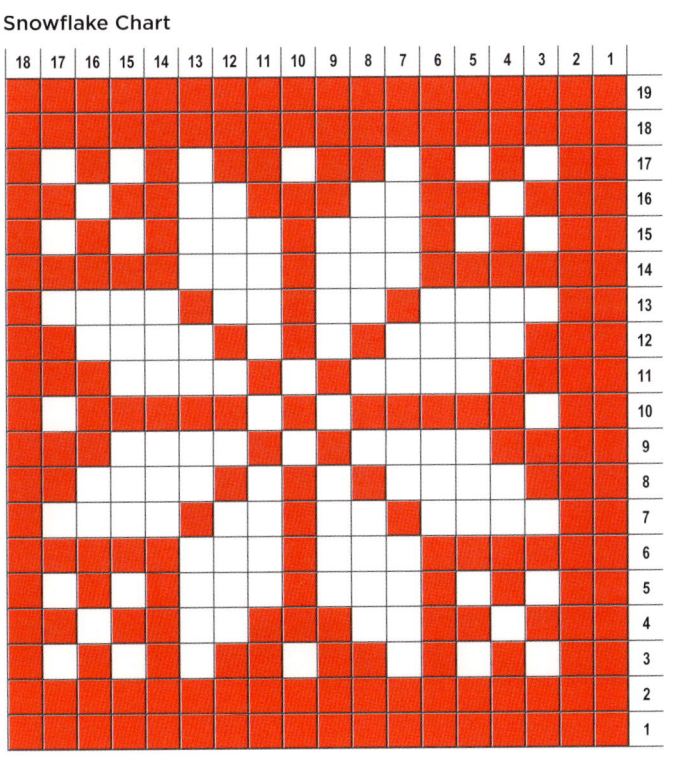

Tree Chart

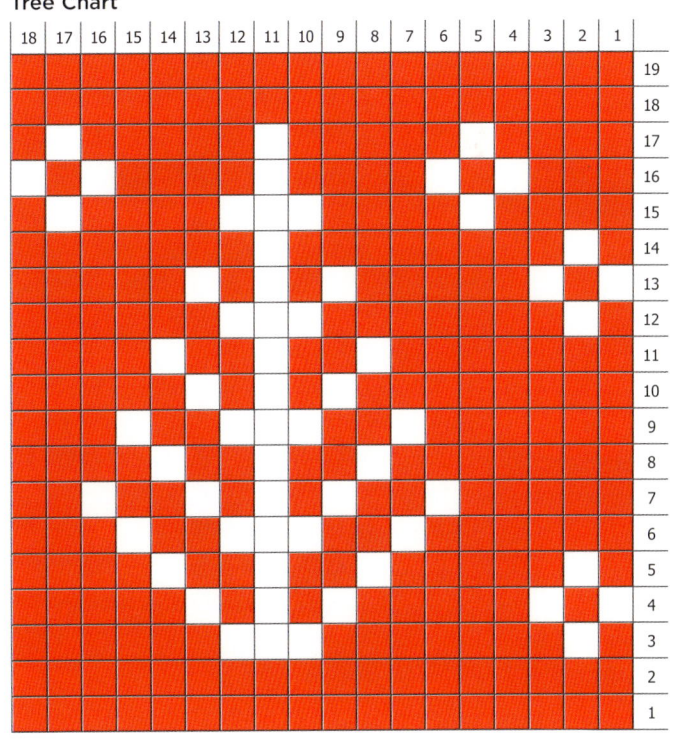

Festive Fair Isle Ornaments

SNOW STAR PILLOW
by Tetiana Otruta

FINISHED MEASUREMENTS
17 (17)" wide, 13 (17)" high, blocked; to fit 16" x 12 (16)" pillow.

YARN
Knit Picks Wool of the Andes Worsted (100% Peruvian Highland Wool; 110 yards/50g): MC Fjord Heather 25647, 3 (4) balls; C1 Clarity 25632, 2 (3) balls

NEEDLES
US 6 (4 mm) 24" circular needle, plus two pairs of the same size needles or one 40" or longer needle for Magic Loop recommended for easier working of first 1", or size to obtain gauge

US 4 (3.5 mm) 24" circular needle, or size to obtain gauge

NOTIONS
Stitch Markers
Yarn Needle
Crochet Hook
7 Buttons; approximately 5/8" (15mm)
16 x 12 (16)" Pillow Form

GAUGE
24 sts and 26 rows = 4" in Colorwork Pattern in the rnd on larger needles, blocked
24 sts and 30 rows = 4" in St st in the rnd on smaller needles, blocked

Snow Star Pillow

Notes:
The Snow Star Pillow is worked seamlessly in the round from the bottom up.
Read Chart A from right to left. The number of repeats for the 16x16" pillow are written in parenthesis where different.
Work the YO made with both strands MC and C1 as one knit st on the next rnd.
The last stitch of the round in the Colorwork section is not shown on the chart or in the written line-by-line instructions. Purl with MC this last stitch in the round, to balance gap in colorwork pattern at the beginning and the end of the rnd.

BO P-wise: P1, *P1, pull the first st on the RH needle over the second st and off the right needle; rep from * to end.

Colorwork Pattern, Chart A (worked in the round over multiples of 26 sts)
Rnd 1: K5 with MC, K3 with C1, K1 with MC, K2 with C1, K3 with MC, K2 with C1, K1 with MC, K3 with C1, K5 with MC, K1 with C1.
Rnds 2 and 26: K1 MC, K3 C1, K2 MC, K1 C1, K3 MC, K2 C1, K1 MC, K2 C1, K3 MC, K1 C1, K2 MC, K3 C1, K2 MC.
Rnds 3 and 25: K1 C1, K1 MC, K3 C1, K4 MC, K1 C1, K1 MC, K3 C1, K1 MC, K1 C1, K4 MC, K3 C1, K1 MC, K1 C1, K1 MC.
Rnds 4 and 24: K2 C1, K1 MC, K3 C1, K2 MC, [K1 C1, K1 MC] 4 times, K1 C1, K2 MC, K3 C1, K1 MC, K2 C1, K1 MC.
Rnds 5 and 23: K3 C1, K4 MC, K1 C1, K1 MC, K1 C1, K5 MC, K1 C1, K1 MC, K1 C1, K4 MC, K3 C1, K1 MC.
Rnds 6 and 22: K1 MC, K2 C1, K3 MC, K1 C1, K1 MC, K1 C1, K3 MC, K1 C1, K3 MC, K1 C1, K1 MC, K1 C1, K3 MC, K2 C1, K2 MC.
Rnds 7 and 21: K2 MC, K1 C1, K2 MC, K1 C1, K1 MC, K1 C1, K1 MC, K1 C1, K3 MC, K3 C1, K3 MC, K1 C1, K1 MC, K1 C1, K2 MC, K1 C1, K2 MC, K1 C1.
Rnds 8 and 20: K1 C1, K3 MC, K1 C1, K1 MC, [K1 C1, K2 MC] 4 times, K1 C1, K1 MC, K1 C1, K3 MC, K2 C1.
Rnds 9 and 19: K3 MC, K1 C1, K1 MC, K1 C1, [K3 MC, K2 C1] 2 times, K3 MC, K1 C1, K1 MC, K1 C1, K3 MC, K1 C1.
Rnds 10 and 18: K2 MC, K1 C1, K1 MC, K1 C1, K4 MC, K3 C1, K1 MC, K3 C1, K4 MC, K1 C1, K1 MC, K1 C1, K3 MC.
Rnds 11 and 17: [K1 MC, K1 C1] 2 times, K2 MC, K3 C1, K1 MC, [K2 C1, K1 MC] 2 times, K3 C1, K2 MC, [K1 C1, K1 MC] 2 times, K1 C1.
Rnds 12 and 16: K1 C1, K1 MC, K1 C1, K4 MC, K3 C1, [K1 MC, K1 C1] 2 times, K1 MC, K3 C1, K4 MC, K1 C1, K1 MC, K2 C1.
Rnds 13 and 15: K2 C1, K3 MC, K1 C1, K2 MC, K3 C1, K3 MC, K3 C1, K2 MC, K1 C1, K3 MC, K2 C1, K1 MC.
Rnd 14: K1 MC, K2 C1, K1 MC, K3 C1, K5 MC, K1 C1, K5 MC, K3 C1, K1 MC, K2 C1, K2 MC.
Rep Rnds 1-26 for pattern.

DIRECTIONS

With larger needle and MC, CO 105 sts using Long Tail cast on method. Move sts onto needle cord. With crochet hook and working yarn, PU and place onto smaller needle 104 sts from CO edge (see Picture). 209 sts.
PM for rnd beginning.
Set-up Rnd: Switch to smaller needles. K208, P1.

Switch to larger needles.
Note: Work in the rnd on two pairs of circular needles or one long circular needle (for Magic Loop) until piece measures at least 1" or it is comfortable to work on one 24" circular needle.
Work Colorwork Pattern Rnd 1 over 208 sts, repeating Chart A or written instructions 8 times around to last st, P1 MC. You may use additional stitch markers between each Colorwork Pattern repeat. Continue as established, working Rnds 1-26 of Chart A 3 (4) times total.

Next Rnd (7 Buttonhole Row): *K5 MC, K3 C1, K1 MC, K2 C1, SKP MC, YO with both strands MC and C1, K1 MC, K2 C1, K1 MC, K3 C1, K4 MC, SKP MC, YO with both strands MC and C1; rep from * 2 additional times, K5 MC, K3 C1, K1 MC, K2 C1, SKP MC, YO with both strands MC and C1, K1 MC, K2 C1, K1 MC, K3 C1, K5 MC, K1 C1, **K5 MC, K3 C1, K1 MC, K2 C1, K3 MC, K2 C1, K1 MC, K3 C1, K5 MC, K1 C1; rep from ** 3 additional times, P1 MC.
Note: Work YO made with both strands of MC and C1 as one knit st on the next rnd.

Cut C1, continue with MC. Switch to smaller needle.
Next Rnd 1: K until 2 sts from end, SKP. 208 sts.
Next Rnd 2: K around.
Next Rnd: BO 104 sts P-wise, K to end. 104 sts.

Continue to work next rows flat.
Rows 1, 3 (WS): P to end.
Row 2 (RS): K to end.
Row 4 (RS): K1, [K2, P2] rep to 3 st from end, K3.
Row 5 (WS): P3, [K2, P2] rep to 1 st from end, P1.
Rep Rows 4-5 seven times more, ending with a WS row.

BO all sts P-wise on RS row.

Finishing

Sew on buttons on the St st part of the flap. Fold flap inside and attach its sides with invisible seams to the pillowcase sides. Stitch up the pillowcase opening to the flap about 0.75" from corner. Weave in yarn ends, block, trim ends after blocking.

Chart A

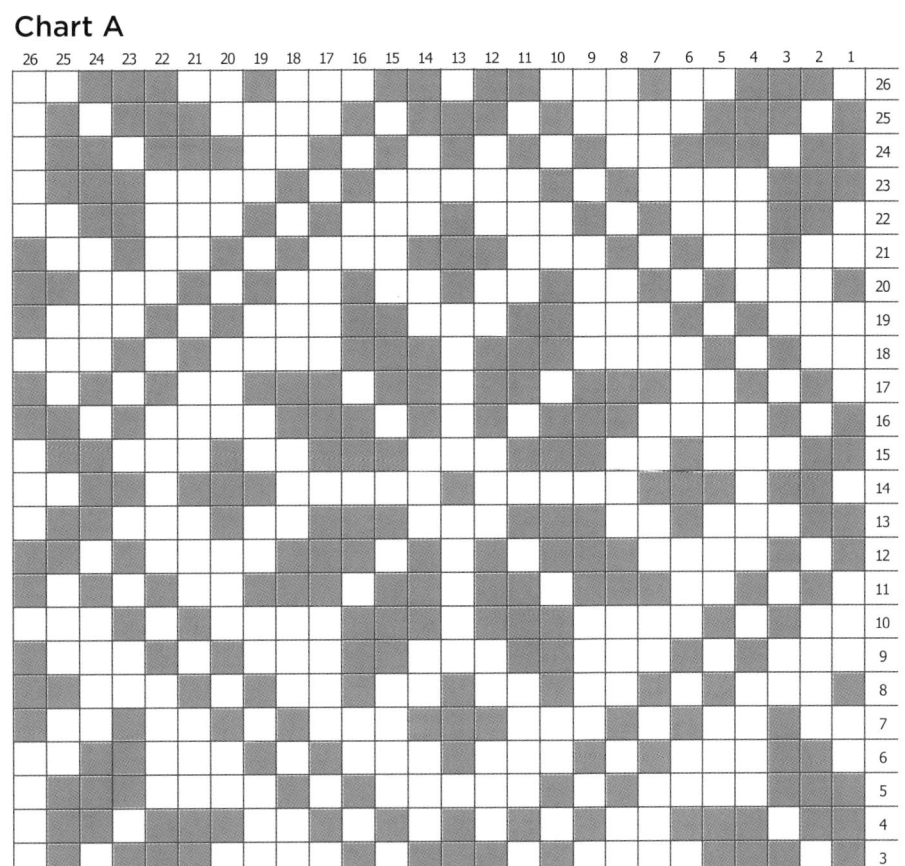
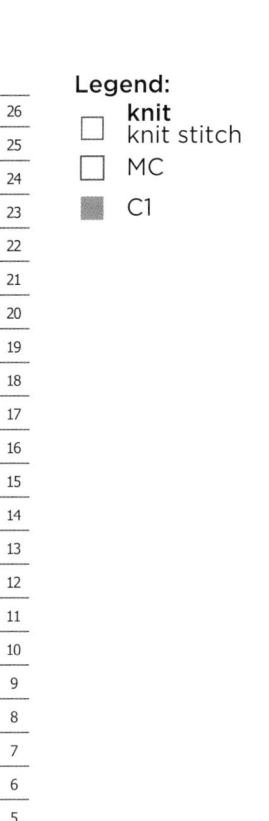

Legend:
- **knit** / knit stitch
- ☐ MC
- ▩ C1

CABLE SWEATER FOR COFFEE MUG

by Margaret Holzmann

FINISHED MEASUREMENTS
11.5" circumference x 4" high

YARN
Knit Picks Comfy Worsted (75% Pima Cotton, 25% Acrylic; 109 yards/50g): Ivory 24162, 1 ball

NEEDLES
US 7 (4.5mm) straight or circular needles, or size to obtain gauge
US 5 (3.75mm) straight or circular needles, or two sizes smaller than size to obtain gauge

NOTIONS
Sewing Needle and matching Thread
Four 3/8" Buttons
Cable Needle
Yarn Needle
12-ounce capacity Mug, approximately 4" high x 10.5 circumference
Fiberfill

GAUGE
18.75 sts and 26 rows = 4" in Sweater Body cable pattern on larger needles, blocked

For pattern support, contact margaret@spinroot.com

Cable Sweater for Coffee Mug

Notes:
The mug sweater is worked flat. A garter stitch placket is worked on each selvedge edge with button holes on the right placket, so that the sweater can be removed for washing. The sleeves are worked flat from top to bottom, the sleeves seams are sewn and the sleeves are stuffed with fiberfill and attached to the sweater front.

Read RS charts rows (odd numbers) from right to left, and WS rows (even numbers) from left to right.

2/2 LC: SL next 2 sts to CN and hold to front, K next 2 sts, K sts from CN.

2/2 RC: SL next 2 sts to CN and hold to back, K next 2 sts, K sts from CN.

DIRECTIONS
Sweater Body
With smaller needles, CO 56 sts. Begin working from Sweater Body chart or written instructions, below. If working from the chart, note needle size changes at Rows 5 and 23.
Row 1 (RS): K4, (P1, K1 TBL) 24 times, K4.
Row 2 (WS): K4, (P1 TBL, K1) 23 times, P1 TBL, K5.
Row 3: K1, K2tog, YO, K1, (P1, K1 TBL) 24 times, K4.
Row 4: K4, (P1 TBL, K1) 6 times, P1 TBL, KFB, (P1 TBL, K1) 12 times, P1 TBL, KFB, (P1 TBL, K1) 3 times, P1 TBL, K5. 58 sts.
Change to larger needles.
Row 5: BO 4, P3, 2/2 LC, K2, (P1, K1 TBL) 2 times, P1, 2/2 LC, K2, P10, 2/2 LC, K2, (P1, K1 TBL) 2 times, P1, 2/2 LC, K2, P3, K4. 54 sts.
Row 6: BO 4, K3, P6, (K1, P1 TBL) 2 times, K1, P6, K10, P6, (K1, P1 TBL) 2 times, K1, P6, K3, CO 4.
Row 7: K4, P1 TBL, P2, K2, 2/2 RC, (P1, K1 TBL) 2 times, P1, K2, 2/2 RC, P10, K2, 2/2 RC, (P1, K1 TBL) 2 times, P1, K2, 2/2 RC, P3, CO 4. 58 sts.
Row 8: K4, K1 TBL, K2, P6, (K1, P1 TBL) 2 times, K1, P6, K10, P6, (K1, P1 TBL) 2 times, K1, P6, K7.
Row 9: K1, K2tog, YO, K1, P3, 2/2 LC, K2, (P1, K1 TBL) 2 times, P1, 2/2 LC, K2, P10, 2/2 LC, K2, (P1, K1 TBL) 2 times, P1, 2/2 LC, K2, P3, K4.
Row 10: K7, P6, (K1, P1 TBL) 2 times, K1, P6, K10, P6, (K1, P1 TBL) 2 times, K1, P6, K7.
Row 11: K4, P3, K2, 2/2 RC, (P1, K1 TBL) 2 times, P1, K2, 2/2 RC, P10, K2, 2/2 RC, (P1, K1 TBL) 2 times, P1, K2, 2/2 RC, P3, K4.
Row 12: Rep Row 10.
Row 13: K4, P3, 2/2 LC, K2, (P1, K1 TBL) 2 times, P1, 2/2 LC, K2, P10, 2/2 LC, K2, (P1, K1 TBL) 2 times, P1, 2/2 LC, K2, P3, K4.
Rows 14 - 17: Rep Rows 10 - 13.
Row 18: Rep Row 10.
Row 19: K1, K2tog, YO, K1, P3, K2, 2/2 RC, (P1, K1 TBL) 2 times, P1, K2, 2/2 RC, P10, K2, 2/2 RC, (P1, K1 TBL) 2 times, P1, K2, 2/2 RC, P3, K4.
Row 20: BO 4, K3, P6, (K1, P1 TBL) 2 times, K1, P6, K10, P6, (K1, P1 TBL) 2 times, K1, P6, K7. 54 sts.
Row 21: BO 4, P3, 2/2 LC, K2, (P1, K1 TBL) 2 times, P1, 2/2 LC, K2, P10, 2/2 LC, K2, (P1, K1 TBL) 2 times, P1, 2/2 LC, K2, P3, CO 4.
Row 22: K4, K1 TBL, K2, P6, (K1, P1 TBL) 2 times, K1, P6, K10, P6, (K1, P1 TBL) 2 times, K1, P6, K3, CO 4. 58 sts.
Change to smaller needles.
Row 23: K4, P1 TBL, (K1 TBL, P1) x 3, K1 TBL, P2tog, (K1 TBL, P1) x 12, K1 TBL, P2tog, (K1 TBL, P1) 6 times, K1 TBL, K4. 56 sts.
Row 24: Rep Row 2.
Row 25: Rep Row 3.
Row 26: Rep Row 2.
BO K-wise, leaving a 28" tail for sewing the top seam.

Arm (make 2)
With larger needles, CO 6 sts. Begin working from Sleeve chart or written instructions, below. If working from the chart, note needle size change at Row 28.
Row 1 (RS): P1, K4, P1.
Row 2 (WS): KFB, P4, KFB. 8 sts.
Row 3: PFB, P1, 2/2 LC, P1, PFB. 10 sts.
Row 4: KFB, K2, P4, K2, KFB. 12 sts.
Row 5: PFB, P3, K4, P3, PFB. 14 sts.
Row 6: K5, P4, K5.
Row 7: P5, 2/2 LC, P5.
Row 8: Rep Row 6.
Row 9: P5, K4, P5.
Row 10: Rep Row 6.
Row 11: P2tog, P3, 2/2 LC, P3, P2tog. 12 sts.
Row 12: K4, P4, K4.
Row 13: P4, K4, P4.
Row 14: Rep Row 12.
Row 15: P4, 2/2 LC, P4.
Rows 16 - 27: Rep Rows 12 - 15.
Change to smaller needles.
Row 28: (P TBL, K1) 6 times.
Row 29: (P1, K1 TBL) 6 times.
Rows 30 - 31: Rep Rows 28 -29.
Row 32: K to end.
Row 33: K2tog 6 times. 6 sts.
Draw yarn through 6 remaining sts, tighten and tie securely. Cut, leaving a 16" tail.

Assembly
Buttons: Place a marker or pin 0.5" from left selvedge edge, and aligning with the vertical positions of of the four button holes. Sew a button at each marked position.

Arms: To sew and stuff an arm, fold the arm lengthwise with WS together, matching selvedge edge sts. Using the 16" tail, whip stitch the selvedge edges together, stuffing the arm with fiberfill, incrementally, as sewing progresses. Arms should be lightly stuffed.

To attach the arms to the mug, put the body of the sweater on the mug and button it. Pin the open tops of the arms to the top-ribbed edge of the sweater body. Both arms are the same so it doesn't matter which is selected as the right or left arm. Position the 'right' arm just to the left of the top button, and position the 'left' arm on the exact opposite position. Pin the open arm seam in place and whip stitch around the opening to attach it to the body of the sweater. For each arm, bend the arm at the 'elbow' and make a few sts to attach the ribbing of the 'wrist' to the belly of the sweater body. Tie off ends securely and weave in loose ends.

Sleeve Chart

Legend:

- ☐ **knit** — RS: knit stitch / WS: purl stitch
- ■ **No Stitch**
- • **purl** — RS: purl stitch / WS: knit stitch
- O **yo** — Yarn Over
- — **bind off** — bind off a st
- + **cast on** — cast on a st
- ~ **purl tbl** — RS: Purl stitch through the back loop / WS: Knit stitch through the back loop
- ⋎ **Purl Front and Back** — purl in front of st and leave st on left needle, then purl again in TBL
- ⁄. **p2tog** — RS: Purl 2 stitches together / WS: Knit 2 stitches together
- B **knit tbl** — Knit stitch through back loop
- ⁄ **k2tog** — RS: Knit two stitches together as one stitch / WS: Purl 2 stitches together
- **c2 over 2 left** — sl 2 to CN, hold in front. k2, k2 from CN
- **c2 over 2 right** — sl2 to CN, hold in back. k2, k2 from CN

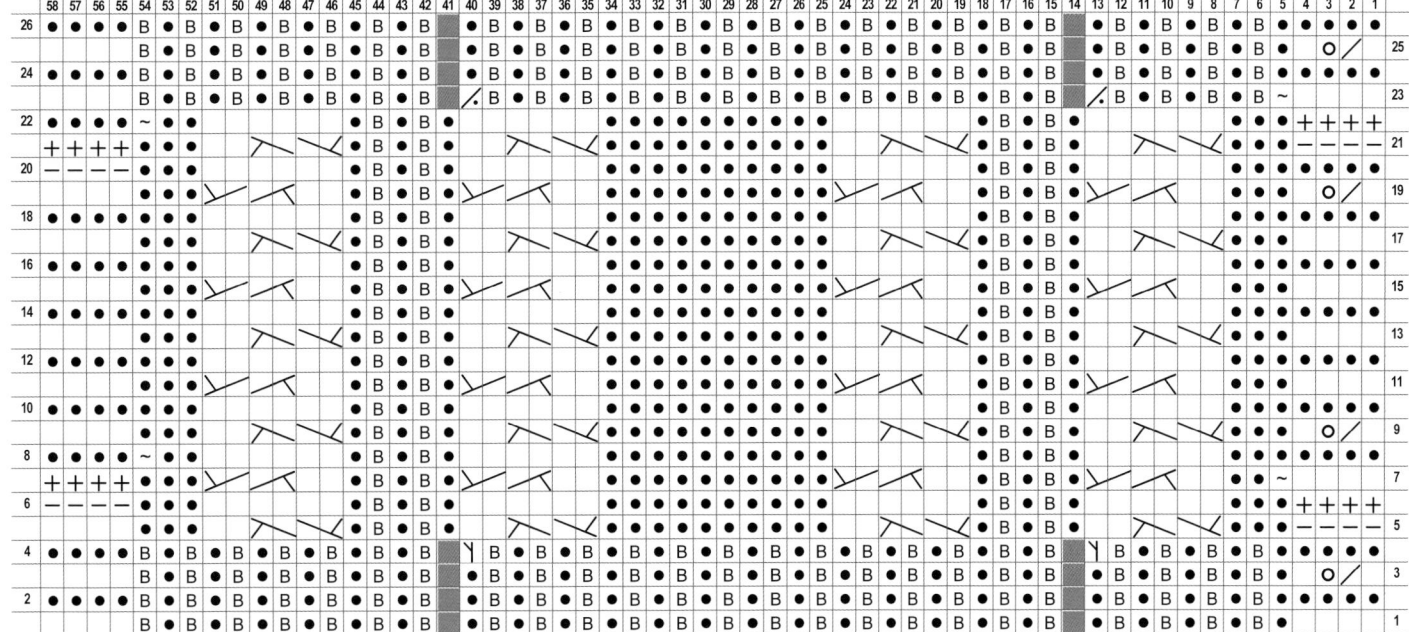

Cable Sweater for Coffee Mug 59

NORDIC STOCKING

by Margaret Mills

FINISHED MEASUREMENTS
7" wide at cuff x 21" long

YARN
Knit Picks Wool of the Andes Worsted (100% Peruvian Highland Wool; 110 yards/50g): MC White 24065, C1 Dove Heather 24077, 2 balls each; C2 Delft Heather 25649, C3 Red 23764; 1 ball each

NEEDLES
US 6 (4mm) DPNs or two 24" circular needles for two circulars technique, or one 32" or longer circular needle for Magic Loop technique, or size to obtain gauge

US 4 (3.5mm) needle in any style for 3-Needle BO, or two sizes smaller than needle to obtain gauge

NOTIONS
Yarn Needle
Stitch Markers (2)
Smooth Waste Yarn, approximately 3' length

GAUGE
24 sts and 29 rows = 4" in stranded St st in the round on larger needles, blocked.
Gauge is not critical for this project, but a change in gauge will affect the finished size and yarn requirements.

For pattern support, contact margaretgracemills@gmail.com

Nordic Stocking

Notes:

This cheery stocking will add Nordic charm to your Christmas décor! Knit in worsted weight wool, the stranded colorwork fabric is firm enough to hold lots of goodies. For all its color, though, it uses only two colors per round. Use duplicate stitch to add initials or a name (up to 7 letters, using the alphabet included) to the top line of snowflakes. If you strand C3 when working Charts A and B, be sure to carry the floats loosely, catching them every four or five stitches. Those stitches can be worked in Duplicate Stitch, if you prefer.

The stocking is worked top-down, with a knitted-in hem and an afterthought heel. The end of round falls at the left edge of the stocking, in the middle of the heel. The pattern for this stocking is made up of two motifs, Chart A and Chart B. Sometimes the stitches represented by grey boxes are knit using C1; sometimes they are knit using C2. Sometimes you start a round with Chart A; sometimes you start with Chart B. Pay attention to both of these distinctions in each section/paragraph of the pattern. Refer to the pictures of the finished stocking for clarification. The charts are followed from bottom to top, reading each row from right to left as a RS row.

Before you start: If you want to add a name to the top of the stocking, cut three 1 yard strands of C3 (or be prepared to pull from the other end of the ball) to use in duplicate stitching.

A tutorial for the Knitted Cast On can be found here: http://tutorials.knitpicks.com/knitted-cast-on/.

Stockinette Stitch (St st, worked in the round)
All Rnds: Knit.

DIRECTIONS

Hem
With MC and using Knitted CO, CO 78 sts. PM for start of rnd. Join to work in the round being careful not to twist sts, and work in St st for 12 rnds.

Next Rnd: (Kfb, K12) to end. 84 sts.
Next Rnd (Turning Rnd): P.

Leg
Next Rnd: Follow Row 14 of Charts (K1 in C3, K13 in MC) across rnd.
Next Rnd: Using MC, C1, and C3, and starting with Chart A, follow Row 1 of Charts, alternating Chart A and Chart B across rnd (ABABAB).
Work across sts, following charts as set through Row 13, omitting C3 in Row 7 (working a plain MC rnd) if you want to add a name to the top of the stocking.

Using the strands of C3 you cut before casting on, use duplicate stitch to add a name or initials onto the front of the stocking, centering the name over the first three motifs of the round. Don't forget to orient the letters correctly, with the live stitches below them!
Weave in all CC yarn ends.

Next Rnd (Hem Rnd): Fold over hem to back of work and hold together with live sts. Following Row 14 of Charts, *K1 in C3, K2tog 1 st from needle tog with 1 loop from CO in MC 13 times; rep from * across rnd.

Next Rnd: Using MC, C2, and C3, and starting with Chart B, follow Row 1 of Charts, alternating Chart B and Chart A across rnd (BABABA).
Work Charts as set through Row 14.
Next Rnd: Using MC, C1, and C3, and starting with Chart A, follow Row 1 of Charts, alternating Chart A and Chart B across rnd (ABABAB).
Work Charts as set through Row 14.
Next Rnd: Using MC, C1, and C3, and starting with Chart B, follow Row 1 of Charts, alternating Chart B and Chart A across rnd (BABABA).
Work Charts as set through Row 14.
Next Rnd: Using MC, C2, and C3, and starting with Chart A, follow Row 1 of Charts, alternating Chart A and Chart B across rnd (ABABAB).
Work Charts as set through Row 14.
Next Rnd: Using MC, C1, and C3, and starting with Chart B, follow Row 1 of Charts, alternating Chart B and Chart A across Rnd (BABABA).
Work Charts as set through Row 13 (not Row 14!). Break C1 yarn.

Heel Placement
Next Rnd: Using MC and C3, follow Row 14 of Charts over the first 64 sts of the rnd.
Using smooth waste yarn, K41 (20 sts to the end of rnd and 21 sts from beginning of next rnd).
Sl all waste yarn sts to LH needle. K41 with MC. Break MC yarn. Sl last 21 sts to LH needle.

Foot
Next Rnd: Using MC, C1, and C3, and starting with Chart A, follow Row 1 of Charts, alternating Chart A and Chart B across rnd (ABABAB).
Work Charts as set through Row 14.
Next Rnd: Using MC, C2, and C3, and starting with Chart B, follow Row 1 of Charts, alternating Chart B and Chart A across rnd (BABABA).
Work Charts as set through Row 14.
Next Rnd: Using MC, C1, and C3, and starting with Chart A, follow Row 1 of Charts, alternating Chart A and Chart B across rnd (ABABAB).
Work Charts as set through Row 14. Break MC yarn.

Toe Setup
Next Rnd: Using C1 and C3, (K1 in C1, K1 in C3) across rnd.

Toe
Next Rnd: (K1 C1, K1 C3) 9 times, SKP C1, PM, K1 C1, K1 C3, K1 C1, K2tog C1, K1 C3, (K1 C1, K1 C3) 17 times, SKP C1, PM, K1 C1, K1 C3, K1 C1, K2tog C1, K1 C3, (K1 C1, K1 C3) 8 times. 80 sts.

Next Rnd: WE, working C1 sts in C1 and C3 sts in C3.
Next Rnd: *WE to 2 sts before marker, SKP using color of next st, SM, K1 C1, K1 C3, K1 C1, K2tog using color of 2nd st on LH needle; rep from * once more, WE to end of rnd. 4 sts dec.

Continue to alternate these two rnds, decreasing every other rnd, 8 more times until 44 sts remain.
WE to marker. K1 C1.

Place next 22 sts on one needle and the 22 sts just worked (including 11 from end of previous rnd and 11 at start of rnd) on a second needle.
Carefully turn stocking inside out.
Hold two needles together. Using smaller needle, work 3-Needle BO as follows: Using C1, K tog 2 sts from front needle with 1 st from back needle. *Using C3, K tog 1 from front needle with 1 from back needle, pass first st on RH needle over second st to bind it off, using C1, K tog 1 from front needle with 1 from back needle, pass first st on RH needle over second st; rep from * until 5 sts remain. Using C3, K tog 1 from front needle with 1 from back needle, pass first st on RH needle over second st, using C1, K tog 1 from front needle with 2 from back needle, pass first st on RH needle over second st.
Break yarn, run through final st and pull snug. Turn stocking RS out.

Heel Setup
Carefully pick out waste yarn. Place 41 sts on larger size needles from top of heel and 40 sts on needles from bottom of heel. 81 sts.
Next Rnd: Starting at the corner of the heel in the back of the stocking, using C1 and C3, work across the bottom of heel sts as follows: (K1 C1, K1 C3) to end of bottom of heel sts. PU 2 sts between bottom and top heel sts, K1TBL C1, K1TBL C3. Work across the top of heel sts as follows: (K1 C1, K1 C3) until 1 st remains in top of heel. K1 C1. PU 1 st between top and bottom heel sts, K1TBL C3. 84 sts.
WE for 19 sts, working C1 sts in C1 and C3 sts in C3, to the fold line at the back of the stocking. This is the start of rnd.

Heel
Follow instructions for Toe.

Hanging Loop
Cut three pieces of MC yarn, each about 12" long. Thread all three pieces through one stitch in the turning row of the hem so that half the length of each piece is on either side of the hem stitch. Fold the strands in half, gather in three groups of two strands and braid for 3". Tie a knot at the end of the braid, and secure to the hem row.

Finishing
Weave in ends, wash and block to diagram.

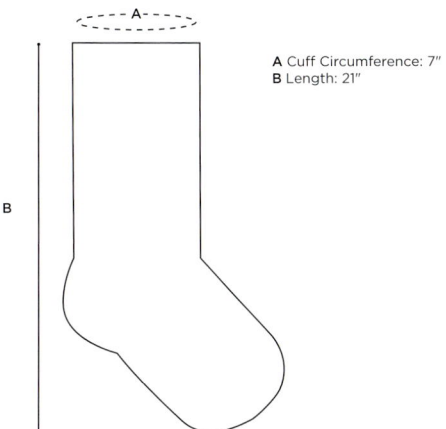

A Cuff Circumference: 7"
B Length: 21"

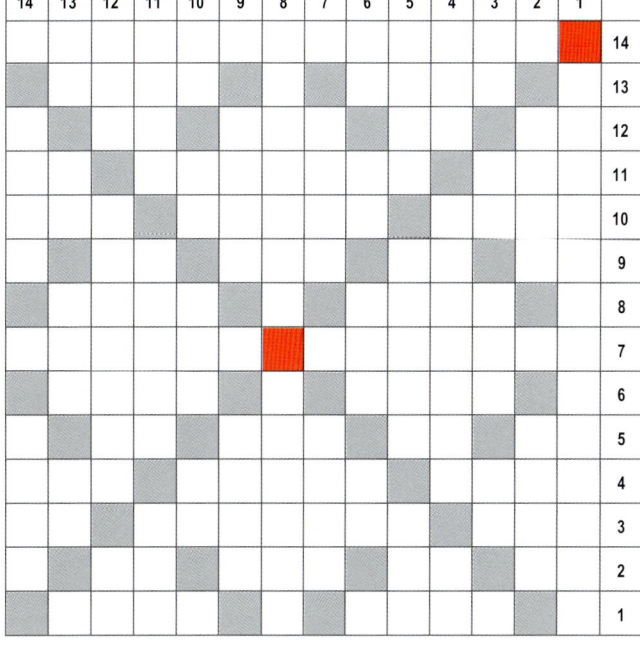

Fill in your name/initials:

41	40	39	38	37	36	35	34	33	32	31	30	29	28	27	26	25	24	23	22	21	20	19	18	17	16	15	14	13	12	11	10	9	8	7	6	5	4	3	2	1	

Nordic Stocking

Alphabet Charts

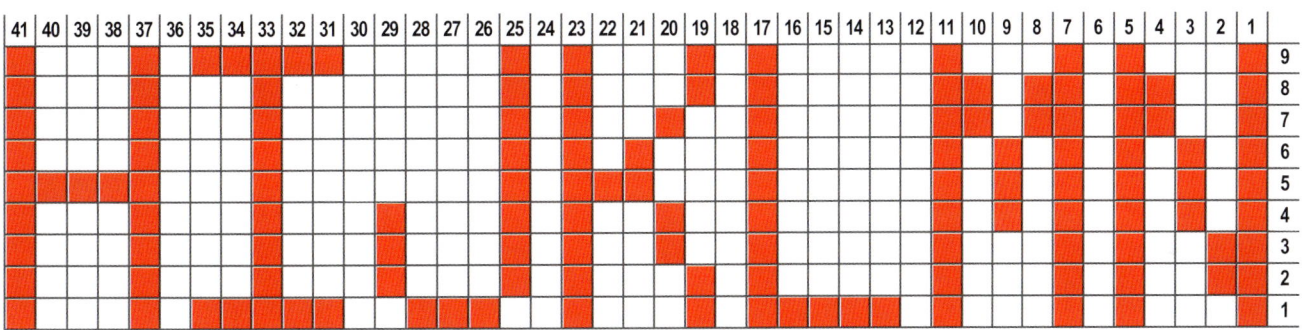

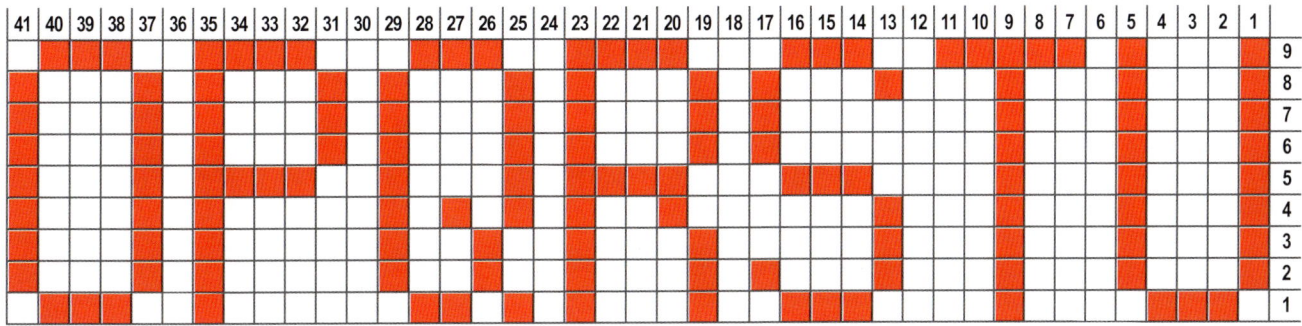

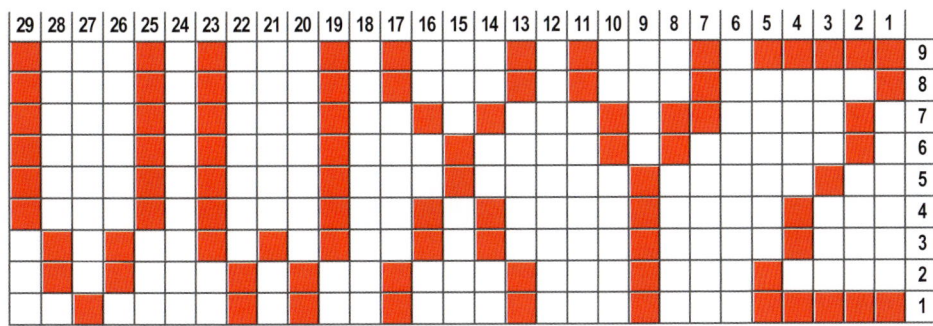

SNOWFLAKE ORNAMENTS

by Margaret Holzmann

FINISHED MEASUREMENTS
4" Square

YARN
Knit Picks Palette (100% Peruvian Highland Wool; 231 yards/50g): MC Turmeric 24251, or Pimento 24246, or Delta 24580; C1 White 23728, 1 skein each

NEEDLES
US 3 (3.25mm) straight or circular needles, or size to obtain gauge

NOTIONS
Yarn Needle
E4 (3.5mm) Crochet Hook
Fiberfill

GAUGE
26 sts and 24 rows = 4" in stranded St st, blocked

Snowflake Ornaments

Notes:

These Fair Isle ornaments feature two different snowflake designs. Each snowflake is formed from two 4" squares, knit flat, then seamed together and stuffed. One style has a white border, and another has a contrasting blanket stitch border. The snowflakes can be adorned with beads, bells or other holiday embellishments.

When working the charts, read RS rows (odd numbers) from right to left, and WS rows (even numbers) from left to right. When a yarn must be carried more than four stitches at the back of the work, twist the MC and contrast yarns every 4th stitch. This practice maintains proper tension in the knitted fabric. For long carries, alternate twist direction to keep the yarns from tangling.

DIRECTIONS

Snowflake 1 (make 1 for each ornament)
Snowflake with blanket stitch border.
In C1, CO 29 sts. Follow Snowflake 1 chart to work the next 29 rows in C1 and MC.
BO P-wise. Cut yarn and tie securely, leaving a 25" tail for sewing squares together. It is not necessary to darn in loose ends.

Snowflake 2 (make 1 for each ornament)
Snowflake with a colored border.
In MC, CO 29 sts. Follow Snowflake 2 chart to work the next 29 rows in C1 and MC. On all rows, after the 3rd st, transitioning between the C1 border and MC, twist the yarns to prevent a hole from forming in the fabric.
BO P-wise. Cut yarn and tie securely, leaving a 25" tail for sewing squares together. It is not necessary to darn in loose ends.

Finishing
Block squares to measurements. Using the long tail, and with WS together, use a whip stitch to seam snowflake squares together, matching tops and bottoms, tucking loose yarn ends to the inside, and catching a single selvedge yarn in each st. When a 1" opening remains, stuff the square with fiberfill, then complete the seam to close.

Snowflake 1: Using MC and the yarn needle, starting at a corner create a blanket stitch edging around all sides.

Using the crochet hook and C1 with yarn held double, create an 8" chain. Using the tails of the 8" chain, tie the chain securely to the center-top edge of the square.

Optional Embellishments
Before sewing squares together, sew white seed beads over the white snowflake motifs to add some sparkle. Add gold or silver bells, a yarn tassel, or a string of beads to the bottom of the ornament.

68   Snowflake Ornaments

Snowflake Chart 1

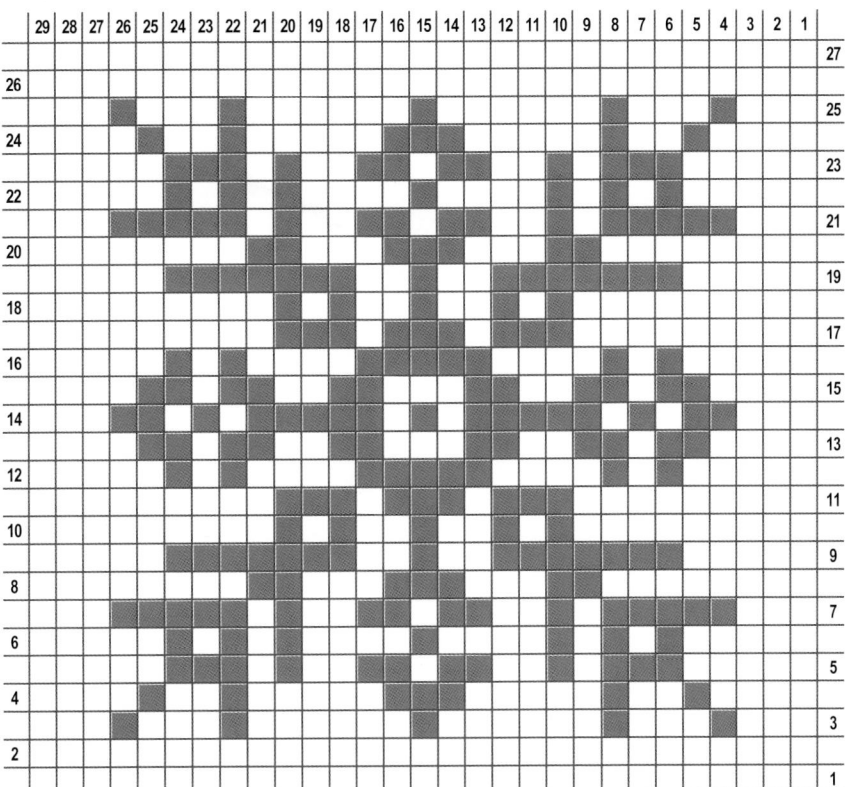

Legend:
- knit — knit stitch
- MC
- C1

Snowflake Chart 2

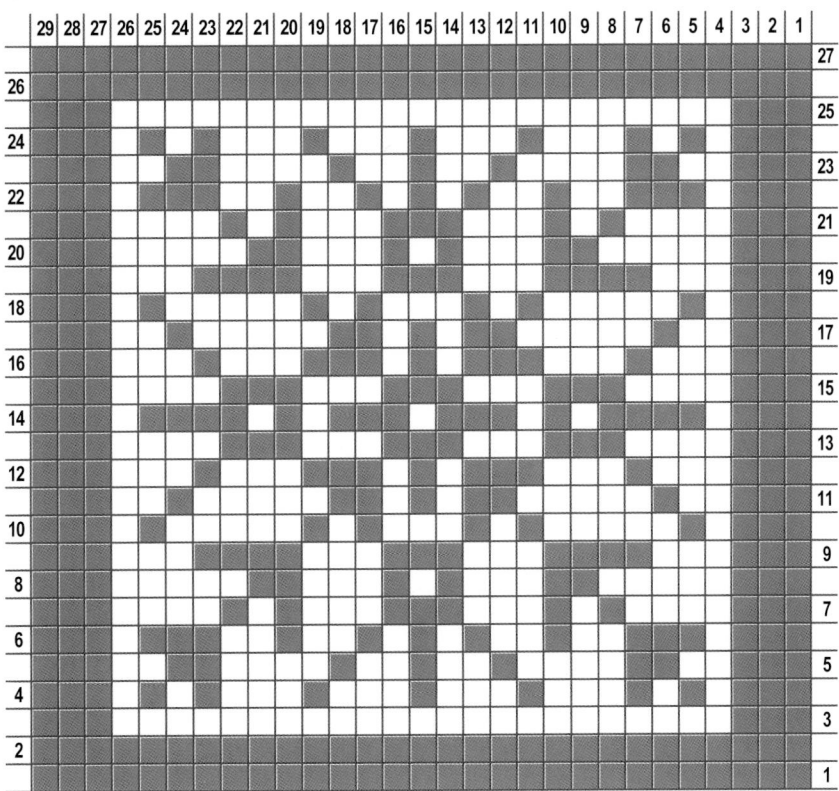

Abbreviations							
BO	bind off	M	marker		stitch	TBL	through back loop
cn	cable needle	M1	make one stitch	RH	right hand	TFL	through front loop
CC	contrast color	M1L	make one left-leaning stitch	rnd(s)	round(s)	tog	together
CDD	Centered double dec			RS	right side	W&T	wrap & turn (see specific instructions in pattern)
CO	cast on	M1R	make one right-leaning stitch	Sk	skip		
cont	continue			Sk2p	sl 1, k2tog, pass slipped stitch over k2tog: 2 sts dec		
dec	decrease(es)	MC	main color			WE	work even
DPN(s)	double pointed needle(s)	P	purl			WS	wrong side
		P2tog	purl 2 sts together	SKP	sl, k, psso: 1 st dec	WYIB	with yarn in back
EOR	every other row	PM	place marker	SL	slip	WYIF	with yarn in front
inc	increase	PFB	purl into the front and back of stitch	SM	slip marker	YO	yarn over
K	knit			SSK	sl, sl, k these 2 sts tog		
K2tog	knit two sts together	PSSO	pass slipped stitch over	SSP	sl, sl, p these 2 sts tog tbl		
KFB	knit into the front and back of stitch	PU	pick up	SSSK	sl, sl, sl, k these 3 sts tog		
		P-wise	purlwise				
K-wise	knitwise	rep	repeat	St st	stockinette stitch		
LH	left hand	Rev St st	reverse stockinette	sts	stitch(es)		

Knit Picks yarn is both luxe and affordable—a seeming contradiction trounced! But it's not just about the pretty colors; we also care deeply about fiber quality and fair labor practices, leaving you with a gorgeously reliable product you'll turn to time and time again.

THIS COLLECTION FEATURES

Palette
Fingering Weight
100% Peruvian Highland Wool

Comfy
Worsted Weight
75% Pima Cotton, 25% Acrylic

Wool Of The Andes Worsted
Worsted Weight
100% Peruvian Highland Wool

Brava Bulky
Bulky Weight
100% Premium Acrylic

Shadow Lace
Lace Weight
100% Merino Wool

Wool Of The Andes Superwash Bulky
Bulky Weight
100% Superwash Wool

Swish
Worsted Weight
100% Superwash Merino Wool

Mighty Stitch
Worsted Weight
80% Acrylic, 20% Superwash Wool

Stroll Sock Yarn
Fingering Weight
75% Superwash Merino Wool, 25% Nyloni

View these beautiful yarns and more at www.KnitPicks.com